50 Crepe Recipes for Home

By: Kelly Johnson

Table of Contents

- Classic French Crepes
- Chocolate Crepes
- Lemon Sugar Crepes
- Nutella Crepes
- Banana Nut Crepes
- Strawberry Cheesecake Crepes
- Blueberry Lemon Crepes
- Raspberry Almond Crepes
- Spinach and Feta Crepes
- Ham and Cheese Crepes
- Smoked Salmon Crepes
- Caprese Crepes (Tomato, Mozzarella, Basil)
- Chicken Alfredo Crepes
- Beef and Mushroom Crepes
- Ratatouille Crepes
- Caramelized Apple Crepes
- Peach Melba Crepes
- Pineapple Coconut Crepes
- Mango Tango Crepes
- Berry Blast Crepes (Assorted Berries)
- Tiramisu Crepes
- Red Velvet Crepes
- S'mores Crepes
- Pumpkin Spice Crepes
- Cinnamon Roll Crepes
- Pecan Pie Crepes
- Maple Bacon Crepes
- Irish Cream Crepes
- Lemon Meringue Crepes
- Black Forest Crepes (Cherry, Chocolate)
- Cannoli Crepes
- Key Lime Pie Crepes
- Chocolate Peanut Butter Cup Crepes
- Bananas Foster Crepes
- Strawberry Shortcake Crepes

- Salted Caramel Pretzel Crepes
- Mint Chocolate Chip Crepes
- Raspberry White Chocolate Crepes
- Lemon Blueberry Mascarpone Crepes
- Apple Cinnamon Streusel Crepes
- Orange Creamsicle Crepes
- Hazelnut Espresso Crepes
- Coconut Lime Crepes
- Pina Colada Crepes
- Chocolate Cherry Cordial Crepes
- Cranberry Orange Crepes
- Almond Joy Crepes
- Raspberry Lemon Cheesecake Crepes
- Chocolate Mint Crepes
- White Chocolate Raspberry Crepes

Classic French Crepes

Ingredients:

- 1 cup all-purpose flour
- 2 large eggs
- 1 1/4 cups whole milk
- 2 tablespoons unsalted butter, melted
- 1 tablespoon granulated sugar (optional)
- 1/4 teaspoon salt
- Butter or oil, for cooking

Instructions:

In a large mixing bowl, whisk together the flour, eggs, milk, melted butter, sugar (if using), and salt until smooth. The batter should be thin and pourable. If it's too thick, you can add a bit more milk to reach the desired consistency.

Heat a non-stick skillet or crepe pan over medium heat. Add a small amount of butter or oil to the pan and swirl it around to coat the bottom evenly.

Once the pan is hot, pour about 1/4 cup of the crepe batter into the center of the pan. Quickly tilt and rotate the pan to spread the batter into a thin, even layer covering the bottom of the pan.

Cook the crepe for about 1-2 minutes, or until the edges start to lightly brown and lift away from the pan. Use a spatula to carefully flip the crepe over and cook for an additional 1-2 minutes on the other side, or until lightly golden.

Transfer the cooked crepe to a plate and cover it with a clean kitchen towel to keep warm while you cook the remaining crepes, repeating the process with the remaining batter.

Serve the crepes warm with your choice of toppings, such as Nutella, jam, fresh fruit, whipped cream, or a sprinkle of powdered sugar. Enjoy your classic French crepes!

Note: Crepes can be made ahead of time and stored in the refrigerator for up to 2 days or frozen for longer storage. Simply stack the cooled crepes between sheets of parchment paper, wrap them tightly in plastic wrap, and store in an airtight container or freezer bag. Reheat gently in a skillet or microwave before serving.

Chocolate Crepes

Ingredients:

- 1 cup all-purpose flour
- 2 tablespoons unsweetened cocoa powder
- 2 large eggs
- 1 1/4 cups whole milk
- 2 tablespoons unsalted butter, melted
- 2 tablespoons granulated sugar
- 1/4 teaspoon salt
- Butter or oil, for cooking

Instructions:

In a large mixing bowl, sift together the flour and cocoa powder to remove any lumps and combine them thoroughly.

In another bowl, whisk together the eggs, milk, melted butter, sugar, and salt until well combined.

Gradually add the wet ingredients to the dry ingredients, whisking continuously until you have a smooth batter. The batter should be thin and pourable. If it's too thick, you can add a bit more milk to reach the desired consistency.

Heat a non-stick skillet or crepe pan over medium heat. Add a small amount of butter or oil to the pan and swirl it around to coat the bottom evenly.

Once the pan is hot, pour about 1/4 cup of the crepe batter into the center of the pan. Quickly tilt and rotate the pan to spread the batter into a thin, even layer covering the bottom of the pan.

Cook the crepe for about 1-2 minutes, or until the edges start to lightly brown and lift away from the pan. Use a spatula to carefully flip the crepe over and cook for an additional 1-2 minutes on the other side, or until lightly golden.

Transfer the cooked crepe to a plate and cover it with a clean kitchen towel to keep warm while you cook the remaining crepes, repeating the process with the remaining batter.

Serve the chocolate crepes warm with your favorite toppings, such as chocolate hazelnut spread, whipped cream, fresh berries, or a sprinkle of powdered sugar. Enjoy your delicious chocolate crepes!

Note: Crepes can be made ahead of time and stored in the refrigerator for up to 2 days or frozen for longer storage. Simply stack the cooled crepes between sheets of parchment paper, wrap them tightly in plastic wrap, and store in an airtight container or freezer bag. Reheat gently in a skillet or microwave before serving.

Lemon Sugar Crepes

Ingredients:

- 1 cup all-purpose flour
- 2 large eggs
- 1 1/4 cups whole milk
- 2 tablespoons unsalted butter, melted
- 2 tablespoons granulated sugar
- Zest of 1 lemon
- 1/4 teaspoon salt
- Butter or oil, for cooking
- Additional granulated sugar, for serving
- Lemon wedges, for serving

Instructions:

In a large mixing bowl, whisk together the flour, eggs, milk, melted butter, sugar, lemon zest, and salt until smooth. The batter should be thin and pourable. If it's too thick, you can add a bit more milk to reach the desired consistency.

Heat a non-stick skillet or crepe pan over medium heat. Add a small amount of butter or oil to the pan and swirl it around to coat the bottom evenly.

Once the pan is hot, pour about 1/4 cup of the crepe batter into the center of the pan. Quickly tilt and rotate the pan to spread the batter into a thin, even layer covering the bottom of the pan.

Cook the crepe for about 1-2 minutes, or until the edges start to lightly brown and lift away from the pan. Use a spatula to carefully flip the crepe over and cook for an additional 1-2 minutes on the other side, or until lightly golden.

Transfer the cooked crepe to a plate and sprinkle with additional granulated sugar while still warm. Fold or roll the crepe and serve with lemon wedges on the side.

Repeat the process with the remaining batter, cooking each crepe and sprinkling with sugar as you go.

Serve the lemon sugar crepes warm as a delightful breakfast or dessert option. Enjoy the bright, citrusy flavor of these delicious crepes!

Note: Crepes can be made ahead of time and stored in the refrigerator for up to 2 days or frozen for longer storage. Simply stack the cooled crepes between sheets of parchment paper, wrap them tightly in plastic wrap, and store in an airtight container or freezer bag. Reheat gently in a skillet or microwave before serving.

Nutella Crepes

Ingredients:

- 1 cup all-purpose flour
- 2 large eggs
- 1 1/4 cups whole milk
- 2 tablespoons unsalted butter, melted
- Pinch of salt
- Butter or oil, for cooking
- Nutella, for filling
- Sliced bananas or strawberries (optional), for filling
- Powdered sugar (optional), for dusting

Instructions:

In a large mixing bowl, whisk together the flour, eggs, milk, melted butter, and salt until smooth. The batter should be thin and pourable. If it's too thick, you can add a bit more milk to reach the desired consistency.

Heat a non-stick skillet or crepe pan over medium heat. Add a small amount of butter or oil to the pan and swirl it around to coat the bottom evenly.

Once the pan is hot, pour about 1/4 cup of the crepe batter into the center of the pan. Quickly tilt and rotate the pan to spread the batter into a thin, even layer covering the bottom of the pan.

Cook the crepe for about 1-2 minutes, or until the edges start to lightly brown and lift away from the pan. Use a spatula to carefully flip the crepe over and cook for an additional 1-2 minutes on the other side, or until lightly golden.

Transfer the cooked crepe to a plate. Spread a generous amount of Nutella over half of the crepe, leaving a border around the edges. If desired, add sliced bananas or strawberries on top of the Nutella.

Fold the crepe in half to cover the Nutella and fillings, then fold it in half again to form a triangle or roll it into a cylinder.

Repeat the process with the remaining batter and fillings, cooking each crepe and filling it with Nutella as you go.

Serve the Nutella crepes warm, dusted with powdered sugar if desired. Enjoy the delicious combination of warm, tender crepes and creamy Nutella filling!

Note: You can customize your Nutella crepes with various fillings such as fresh fruit, whipped cream, nuts, or even a drizzle of chocolate sauce. Be creative and make them your own!

Banana Nut Crepes

Ingredients:

For the crepes:

- 1 cup all-purpose flour
- 2 large eggs
- 1 1/4 cups whole milk
- 2 tablespoons unsalted butter, melted
- Pinch of salt
- Butter or oil, for cooking

For the filling:

- 2 ripe bananas, sliced
- 1/4 cup chopped nuts (such as walnuts or pecans)
- 1/4 cup Nutella or chocolate hazelnut spread
- Powdered sugar, for dusting (optional)
- Maple syrup, for serving (optional)

Instructions:

In a large mixing bowl, whisk together the flour, eggs, milk, melted butter, and salt until smooth. The batter should be thin and pourable. If it's too thick, you can add a bit more milk to reach the desired consistency.

Heat a non-stick skillet or crepe pan over medium heat. Add a small amount of butter or oil to the pan and swirl it around to coat the bottom evenly.

Once the pan is hot, pour about 1/4 cup of the crepe batter into the center of the pan. Quickly tilt and rotate the pan to spread the batter into a thin, even layer covering the bottom of the pan.

Cook the crepe for about 1-2 minutes, or until the edges start to lightly brown and lift away from the pan. Use a spatula to carefully flip the crepe over and cook for an additional 1-2 minutes on the other side, or until lightly golden.

Transfer the cooked crepe to a plate. Spread a thin layer of Nutella or chocolate hazelnut spread over the surface of the crepe.

Place sliced bananas and chopped nuts over one half of the crepe.

Fold the crepe in half to cover the banana and nut filling, then fold it in half again to form a triangle or roll it into a cylinder.

Repeat the process with the remaining batter and filling, cooking each crepe and filling it with bananas and nuts as you go.
Serve the banana nut crepes warm, dusted with powdered sugar if desired and drizzled with maple syrup for extra sweetness. Enjoy the delightful combination of tender crepes, creamy Nutella, and crunchy nuts!

Strawberry Cheesecake Crepes

Ingredients:

For the crepes:

- 1 cup all-purpose flour
- 2 large eggs
- 1 1/4 cups whole milk
- 2 tablespoons unsalted butter, melted
- Pinch of salt
- Butter or oil, for cooking

For the cheesecake filling:

- 8 oz (225g) cream cheese, softened
- 1/4 cup powdered sugar
- 1 teaspoon vanilla extract
- 1 cup sliced strawberries

For the topping:

- Additional sliced strawberries
- Whipped cream
- Graham cracker crumbs

Instructions:

In a large mixing bowl, whisk together the flour, eggs, milk, melted butter, and salt until smooth. The batter should be thin and pourable. If it's too thick, you can add a bit more milk to reach the desired consistency.

Heat a non-stick skillet or crepe pan over medium heat. Add a small amount of butter or oil to the pan and swirl it around to coat the bottom evenly.

Once the pan is hot, pour about 1/4 cup of the crepe batter into the center of the pan. Quickly tilt and rotate the pan to spread the batter into a thin, even layer covering the bottom of the pan.

Cook the crepe for about 1-2 minutes, or until the edges start to lightly brown and lift away from the pan. Use a spatula to carefully flip the crepe over and cook for an additional 1-2 minutes on the other side, or until lightly golden.

Transfer the cooked crepe to a plate and set aside.

In a mixing bowl, beat the softened cream cheese, powdered sugar, and vanilla extract until smooth and creamy.

Spread a generous spoonful of the cheesecake filling onto one half of the crepe.

Arrange sliced strawberries over the cheesecake filling.

Fold the crepe in half to cover the cheesecake and strawberry filling, then fold it in half again to form a triangle or roll it into a cylinder.

Repeat the process with the remaining crepes and filling.

Serve the strawberry cheesecake crepes topped with additional sliced strawberries, a dollop of whipped cream, and a sprinkle of graham cracker crumbs for a delightful touch of cheesecake crust flavor.

Enjoy these indulgent crepes as a decadent breakfast or dessert treat!

Blueberry Lemon Crepes

Ingredients:

For the crepes:

- 1 cup all-purpose flour
- 2 large eggs
- 1 1/4 cups whole milk
- 2 tablespoons unsalted butter, melted
- Zest of 1 lemon
- Pinch of salt
- Butter or oil, for cooking

For the blueberry filling:

- 1 1/2 cups fresh blueberries
- 2 tablespoons granulated sugar
- 1 tablespoon lemon juice
- 1 teaspoon cornstarch

For the lemon cream cheese filling:

- 4 oz (115g) cream cheese, softened
- 1/4 cup powdered sugar
- Zest of 1 lemon
- 1 tablespoon lemon juice

Instructions:

In a large mixing bowl, whisk together the flour, eggs, milk, melted butter, lemon zest, and salt until smooth. The batter should be thin and pourable. If it's too thick, you can add a bit more milk to reach the desired consistency.

Heat a non-stick skillet or crepe pan over medium heat. Add a small amount of butter or oil to the pan and swirl it around to coat the bottom evenly.

Once the pan is hot, pour about 1/4 cup of the crepe batter into the center of the pan. Quickly tilt and rotate the pan to spread the batter into a thin, even layer covering the bottom of the pan.

Cook the crepe for about 1-2 minutes, or until the edges start to lightly brown and lift away from the pan. Use a spatula to carefully flip the crepe over and cook for an additional 1-2 minutes on the other side, or until lightly golden.

Transfer the cooked crepe to a plate and set aside.

In a small saucepan, combine the fresh blueberries, granulated sugar, lemon juice, and cornstarch. Cook over medium heat, stirring occasionally, until the blueberries soften and release their juices, and the sauce thickens slightly, about 5 minutes. Remove from heat and let cool slightly.

In a mixing bowl, beat the softened cream cheese, powdered sugar, lemon zest, and lemon juice until smooth and creamy.

Spread a generous spoonful of the lemon cream cheese filling onto one half of the crepe.

Spoon some of the blueberry filling over the lemon cream cheese filling.

Fold the crepe in half to cover the fillings, then fold it in half again to form a triangle or roll it into a cylinder.

Repeat the process with the remaining crepes and fillings.

Serve the blueberry lemon crepes warm and enjoy the delightful combination of tender crepes, tangy lemon cream cheese filling, and sweet blueberry sauce. These crepes make for a delicious breakfast or dessert option, perfect for any occasion!

Raspberry Almond Crepes

Ingredients:

For the crepes:

- 1 cup all-purpose flour
- 2 large eggs
- 1 1/4 cups whole milk
- 2 tablespoons unsalted butter, melted
- Pinch of salt
- Butter or oil, for cooking

For the almond cream filling:

- 4 oz (115g) cream cheese, softened
- 1/4 cup powdered sugar
- 1/2 teaspoon almond extract
- 1/4 cup sliced almonds, toasted

For the raspberry sauce:

- 1 cup fresh raspberries
- 2 tablespoons granulated sugar
- 1 tablespoon water

Instructions:

In a large mixing bowl, whisk together the flour, eggs, milk, melted butter, and salt until smooth. The batter should be thin and pourable. If it's too thick, you can add a bit more milk to reach the desired consistency.

Heat a non-stick skillet or crepe pan over medium heat. Add a small amount of butter or oil to the pan and swirl it around to coat the bottom evenly.

Once the pan is hot, pour about 1/4 cup of the crepe batter into the center of the pan. Quickly tilt and rotate the pan to spread the batter into a thin, even layer covering the bottom of the pan.

Cook the crepe for about 1-2 minutes, or until the edges start to lightly brown and lift away from the pan. Use a spatula to carefully flip the crepe over and cook for an additional 1-2 minutes on the other side, or until lightly golden.

Transfer the cooked crepe to a plate and set aside.

In a mixing bowl, beat the softened cream cheese, powdered sugar, and almond extract until smooth and creamy. Stir in the toasted sliced almonds.

Spread a generous spoonful of the almond cream filling onto one half of the crepe.

Fold the crepe in half to cover the almond cream filling, then fold it in half again to form a triangle or roll it into a cylinder.

In a small saucepan, combine the fresh raspberries, granulated sugar, and water. Cook over medium heat, stirring occasionally, until the raspberries break down and the sauce thickens slightly, about 5 minutes. Remove from heat and let cool slightly.

Drizzle the raspberry sauce over the filled crepes.

Serve the raspberry almond crepes warm and enjoy the delightful combination of tender crepes, creamy almond filling, and tangy raspberry sauce.

These crepes make for a delicious breakfast or dessert option, perfect for any occasion!

Spinach and Feta Crepes

Ingredients:

For the crepes:

- 1 cup all-purpose flour
- 2 large eggs
- 1 1/4 cups whole milk
- 2 tablespoons unsalted butter, melted
- Pinch of salt
- Butter or oil, for cooking

For the filling:

- 2 cups fresh spinach leaves, chopped
- 1/2 cup crumbled feta cheese
- 1/4 cup chopped sun-dried tomatoes (optional)
- 2 cloves garlic, minced
- Salt and pepper to taste
- Olive oil for sautéing

Instructions:

In a large mixing bowl, whisk together the flour, eggs, milk, melted butter, and salt until smooth. The batter should be thin and pourable. If it's too thick, you can add a bit more milk to reach the desired consistency.

Heat a non-stick skillet or crepe pan over medium heat. Add a small amount of butter or oil to the pan and swirl it around to coat the bottom evenly.

Once the pan is hot, pour about 1/4 cup of the crepe batter into the center of the pan. Quickly tilt and rotate the pan to spread the batter into a thin, even layer covering the bottom of the pan.

Cook the crepe for about 1-2 minutes, or until the edges start to lightly brown and lift away from the pan. Use a spatula to carefully flip the crepe over and cook for an additional 1-2 minutes on the other side, or until lightly golden.

Transfer the cooked crepe to a plate and set aside.

In a skillet, heat some olive oil over medium heat. Add the minced garlic and sauté until fragrant, about 1 minute.

Add the chopped spinach to the skillet and cook until wilted, about 2-3 minutes. Season with salt and pepper to taste.

Place a portion of the cooked spinach mixture onto one half of the crepe.

Sprinkle crumbled feta cheese and chopped sun-dried tomatoes (if using) over the spinach mixture.

Fold the crepe in half to cover the filling, then fold it in half again to form a triangle or roll it into a cylinder.

Repeat the process with the remaining crepes and filling.

Serve the spinach and feta crepes warm as a savory breakfast or brunch option.

Enjoy the delicious combination of tender crepes filled with savory spinach, tangy feta cheese, and aromatic garlic!

Ham and Cheese Crepes

Ingredients:

For the crepes:

- 1 cup all-purpose flour
- 2 large eggs
- 1 1/4 cups whole milk
- 2 tablespoons unsalted butter, melted
- Pinch of salt
- Butter or oil, for cooking

For the filling:

- 1 cup diced cooked ham
- 1 cup shredded cheese (such as Swiss, cheddar, or Gruyère)
- 1/4 cup chopped fresh parsley (optional)
- Salt and pepper to taste

Instructions:

In a large mixing bowl, whisk together the flour, eggs, milk, melted butter, and salt until smooth. The batter should be thin and pourable. If it's too thick, you can add a bit more milk to reach the desired consistency.

Heat a non-stick skillet or crepe pan over medium heat. Add a small amount of butter or oil to the pan and swirl it around to coat the bottom evenly.

Once the pan is hot, pour about 1/4 cup of the crepe batter into the center of the pan. Quickly tilt and rotate the pan to spread the batter into a thin, even layer covering the bottom of the pan.

Cook the crepe for about 1-2 minutes, or until the edges start to lightly brown and lift away from the pan. Use a spatula to carefully flip the crepe over and cook for an additional 1-2 minutes on the other side, or until lightly golden.

Transfer the cooked crepe to a plate and set aside.

In a mixing bowl, combine the diced ham, shredded cheese, and chopped fresh parsley (if using). Season with salt and pepper to taste.

Place a portion of the ham and cheese mixture onto one half of the crepe.

Fold the crepe in half to cover the filling, then fold it in half again to form a triangle or roll it into a cylinder.

Repeat the process with the remaining crepes and filling.
Serve the ham and cheese crepes warm as a savory breakfast or brunch option.
Enjoy the delicious combination of tender crepes filled with savory ham and melted cheese!

Smoked Salmon Crepes

Ingredients:

For the crepes:

- 1 cup all-purpose flour
- 2 large eggs
- 1 1/4 cups whole milk
- 2 tablespoons unsalted butter, melted
- Pinch of salt
- Butter or oil, for cooking

For the filling:

- 4 oz (115g) smoked salmon slices
- 4 oz (115g) cream cheese, softened
- 2 tablespoons chopped fresh dill
- 1 tablespoon capers (optional)
- Lemon wedges, for serving

Instructions:

In a large mixing bowl, whisk together the flour, eggs, milk, melted butter, and salt until smooth. The batter should be thin and pourable. If it's too thick, you can add a bit more milk to reach the desired consistency.

Heat a non-stick skillet or crepe pan over medium heat. Add a small amount of butter or oil to the pan and swirl it around to coat the bottom evenly.

Once the pan is hot, pour about 1/4 cup of the crepe batter into the center of the pan. Quickly tilt and rotate the pan to spread the batter into a thin, even layer covering the bottom of the pan.

Cook the crepe for about 1-2 minutes, or until the edges start to lightly brown and lift away from the pan. Use a spatula to carefully flip the crepe over and cook for an additional 1-2 minutes on the other side, or until lightly golden.

Transfer the cooked crepe to a plate and set aside.

In a small mixing bowl, combine the softened cream cheese and chopped fresh dill.

Spread a generous spoonful of the dill cream cheese mixture onto one half of the crepe.
Place a few slices of smoked salmon on top of the cream cheese mixture.
Sprinkle some capers (if using) over the smoked salmon.
Fold the crepe in half to cover the filling, then fold it in half again to form a triangle or roll it into a cylinder.
Repeat the process with the remaining crepes and filling.
Serve the smoked salmon crepes warm, with lemon wedges on the side for squeezing over the top.
Enjoy these elegant and flavorful crepes as a delightful breakfast or brunch option!

Caprese Crepes (Tomato, Mozzarella, Basil)

Ingredients:

For the crepes:

- 1 cup all-purpose flour
- 2 large eggs
- 1 1/4 cups whole milk
- 2 tablespoons unsalted butter, melted
- Pinch of salt
- Butter or oil, for cooking

For the filling:

- 2 ripe tomatoes, thinly sliced
- 8 oz (225g) fresh mozzarella cheese, sliced
- 1/2 cup fresh basil leaves
- Balsamic glaze (optional), for drizzling

Instructions:

In a large mixing bowl, whisk together the flour, eggs, milk, melted butter, and salt until smooth. The batter should be thin and pourable. If it's too thick, you can add a bit more milk to reach the desired consistency.
Heat a non-stick skillet or crepe pan over medium heat. Add a small amount of butter or oil to the pan and swirl it around to coat the bottom evenly.
Once the pan is hot, pour about 1/4 cup of the crepe batter into the center of the pan. Quickly tilt and rotate the pan to spread the batter into a thin, even layer covering the bottom of the pan.
Cook the crepe for about 1-2 minutes, or until the edges start to lightly brown and lift away from the pan. Use a spatula to carefully flip the crepe over and cook for an additional 1-2 minutes on the other side, or until lightly golden.
Transfer the cooked crepe to a plate and set aside.
Arrange a few slices of tomato, mozzarella cheese, and fresh basil leaves on one half of the crepe.
Drizzle with balsamic glaze if desired.

Fold the crepe in half to cover the filling, then fold it in half again to form a triangle or roll it into a cylinder.

Repeat the process with the remaining crepes and filling.

Serve the Caprese crepes warm as a delicious and elegant breakfast or brunch option.

Enjoy the classic combination of ripe tomatoes, creamy mozzarella cheese, and fragrant basil wrapped in tender crepes!

Chicken Alfredo Crepes

Ingredients:

For the crepes:

- 1 cup all-purpose flour
- 2 large eggs
- 1 1/4 cups whole milk
- 2 tablespoons unsalted butter, melted
- Pinch of salt
- Butter or oil, for cooking

For the filling:

- 2 cups cooked chicken breast, diced or shredded
- 1 cup Alfredo sauce (homemade or store-bought)
- 1/2 cup grated Parmesan cheese
- 1/4 cup chopped fresh parsley (optional)
- Salt and pepper to taste

Instructions:

In a large mixing bowl, whisk together the flour, eggs, milk, melted butter, and salt until smooth. The batter should be thin and pourable. If it's too thick, you can add a bit more milk to reach the desired consistency.

Heat a non-stick skillet or crepe pan over medium heat. Add a small amount of butter or oil to the pan and swirl it around to coat the bottom evenly.

Once the pan is hot, pour about 1/4 cup of the crepe batter into the center of the pan. Quickly tilt and rotate the pan to spread the batter into a thin, even layer covering the bottom of the pan.

Cook the crepe for about 1-2 minutes, or until the edges start to lightly brown and lift away from the pan. Use a spatula to carefully flip the crepe over and cook for an additional 1-2 minutes on the other side, or until lightly golden.

Transfer the cooked crepe to a plate and set aside.

In a mixing bowl, combine the cooked chicken breast, Alfredo sauce, grated Parmesan cheese, and chopped fresh parsley (if using). Season with salt and pepper to taste.

Spoon a portion of the chicken Alfredo mixture onto one half of the crepe.
Fold the crepe in half to cover the filling, then fold it in half again to form a triangle or roll it into a cylinder.
Repeat the process with the remaining crepes and filling.
Serve the chicken Alfredo crepes warm as a hearty and satisfying meal.
Enjoy the creamy and flavorful combination of tender crepes filled with savory chicken and Alfredo sauce!

Beef and Mushroom Crepes

Ingredients:

For the crepes:

- 1 cup all-purpose flour
- 2 large eggs
- 1 1/4 cups whole milk
- 2 tablespoons unsalted butter, melted
- Pinch of salt
- Butter or oil, for cooking

For the filling:

- 1 lb (450g) ground beef
- 1 cup sliced mushrooms
- 1 small onion, finely chopped
- 2 cloves garlic, minced
- 2 tablespoons tomato paste
- 1/2 cup beef broth
- 1 teaspoon Worcestershire sauce
- 1/2 teaspoon dried thyme
- Salt and pepper to taste
- 2 tablespoons chopped fresh parsley (optional)

Instructions:

In a large mixing bowl, whisk together the flour, eggs, milk, melted butter, and salt until smooth. The batter should be thin and pourable. If it's too thick, you can add a bit more milk to reach the desired consistency.

Heat a non-stick skillet or crepe pan over medium heat. Add a small amount of butter or oil to the pan and swirl it around to coat the bottom evenly.

Once the pan is hot, pour about 1/4 cup of the crepe batter into the center of the pan. Quickly tilt and rotate the pan to spread the batter into a thin, even layer covering the bottom of the pan.

Cook the crepe for about 1-2 minutes, or until the edges start to lightly brown and lift away from the pan. Use a spatula to carefully flip the crepe over and cook for an additional 1-2 minutes on the other side, or until lightly golden. Transfer the cooked crepe to a plate and set aside. Repeat with the remaining batter.

In a skillet, cook the ground beef over medium heat until browned. Drain excess fat if necessary.

Add the sliced mushrooms, chopped onion, and minced garlic to the skillet with the ground beef. Cook until the vegetables are softened.

Stir in the tomato paste, beef broth, Worcestershire sauce, dried thyme, salt, and pepper. Simmer for a few minutes until the sauce thickens slightly.

Spoon a portion of the beef and mushroom mixture onto one half of each crepe. Fold the crepe in half to cover the filling, then fold it in half again to form a triangle or roll it into a cylinder.

Repeat the process with the remaining crepes and filling.

Sprinkle with chopped fresh parsley if desired before serving.

Serve the beef and mushroom crepes warm as a delicious and satisfying meal. Enjoy the savory combination of tender crepes filled with flavorful beef and mushrooms!

Ratatouille Crepes

Ingredients:

For the crepes:

- 1 cup all-purpose flour
- 2 large eggs
- 1 1/4 cups whole milk
- 2 tablespoons unsalted butter, melted
- Pinch of salt
- Butter or oil, for cooking

For the ratatouille filling:

- 1 small eggplant, diced
- 1 small zucchini, diced
- 1 small yellow squash, diced
- 1 red bell pepper, diced
- 1 yellow bell pepper, diced
- 1 onion, diced
- 2 cloves garlic, minced
- 2 tablespoons tomato paste
- 1 (14 oz) can diced tomatoes
- 1 teaspoon dried thyme
- 1 teaspoon dried oregano
- Salt and pepper to taste
- Olive oil for cooking

Instructions:

In a large mixing bowl, whisk together the flour, eggs, milk, melted butter, and salt until smooth. The batter should be thin and pourable. If it's too thick, you can add a bit more milk to reach the desired consistency.

Heat a non-stick skillet or crepe pan over medium heat. Add a small amount of butter or oil to the pan and swirl it around to coat the bottom evenly.

Once the pan is hot, pour about 1/4 cup of the crepe batter into the center of the pan. Quickly tilt and rotate the pan to spread the batter into a thin, even layer covering the bottom of the pan.

Cook the crepe for about 1-2 minutes, or until the edges start to lightly brown and lift away from the pan. Use a spatula to carefully flip the crepe over and cook for an additional 1-2 minutes on the other side, or until lightly golden.

Transfer the cooked crepe to a plate and set aside. Repeat with the remaining batter.

In a large skillet, heat some olive oil over medium heat. Add the diced eggplant, zucchini, yellow squash, bell peppers, onion, and minced garlic. Cook, stirring occasionally, until the vegetables are softened, about 8-10 minutes.

Stir in the tomato paste, diced tomatoes (with their juices), dried thyme, and dried oregano. Season with salt and pepper to taste. Cook for another 5-7 minutes, or until the flavors are well combined and the ratatouille mixture has thickened slightly.

Spoon a portion of the ratatouille filling onto one half of each crepe.

Fold the crepe in half to cover the filling, then fold it in half again to form a triangle or roll it into a cylinder.

Repeat the process with the remaining crepes and filling.

Serve the ratatouille crepes warm as a flavorful and nutritious meal option.

Enjoy the delicious combination of tender crepes filled with hearty and savory ratatouille!

Caramelized Apple Crepes

Ingredients:

For the crepes:

- 1 cup all-purpose flour
- 2 large eggs
- 1 1/4 cups whole milk
- 2 tablespoons unsalted butter, melted
- Pinch of salt
- Butter or oil, for cooking

For the caramelized apple filling:

- 3-4 medium apples, peeled, cored, and thinly sliced
- 3 tablespoons unsalted butter
- 1/4 cup brown sugar
- 1 teaspoon ground cinnamon
- 1/4 teaspoon ground nutmeg
- Pinch of salt

For serving (optional):

- Whipped cream or vanilla ice cream
- Caramel sauce or powdered sugar for garnish

Instructions:

In a large mixing bowl, whisk together the flour, eggs, milk, melted butter, and salt until smooth. The batter should be thin and pourable. If it's too thick, you can add a bit more milk to reach the desired consistency.

Heat a non-stick skillet or crepe pan over medium heat. Add a small amount of butter or oil to the pan and swirl it around to coat the bottom evenly.

Once the pan is hot, pour about 1/4 cup of the crepe batter into the center of the pan. Quickly tilt and rotate the pan to spread the batter into a thin, even layer covering the bottom of the pan.

Cook the crepe for about 1-2 minutes, or until the edges start to lightly brown and lift away from the pan. Use a spatula to carefully flip the crepe over and cook for an additional 1-2 minutes on the other side, or until lightly golden.

Transfer the cooked crepe to a plate and set aside. Repeat with the remaining batter.

In a large skillet, melt the butter over medium heat. Add the sliced apples and cook, stirring occasionally, until they start to soften, about 5 minutes.

Sprinkle the brown sugar, ground cinnamon, ground nutmeg, and a pinch of salt over the apples. Stir well to coat the apples evenly.

Continue cooking the apples, stirring occasionally, until they are tender and caramelized, about 5-7 minutes more. Remove from heat.

Spoon a portion of the caramelized apple filling onto one half of each crepe. Fold the crepe in half to cover the filling, then fold it in half again to form a triangle or roll it into a cylinder.

Repeat the process with the remaining crepes and filling.

Serve the caramelized apple crepes warm, topped with whipped cream or vanilla ice cream if desired. Drizzle with caramel sauce or sprinkle with powdered sugar for an extra touch of sweetness.

Enjoy the delightful combination of tender crepes filled with warm, caramelized apples—a perfect treat for breakfast or dessert!

Peach Melba Crepes

Ingredients:

For the crepes:

- 1 cup all-purpose flour
- 2 large eggs
- 1 1/4 cups whole milk
- 2 tablespoons unsalted butter, melted
- Pinch of salt
- Butter or oil, for cooking

For the peach filling:

- 2 ripe peaches, peeled, pitted, and sliced
- 2 tablespoons granulated sugar
- 1 tablespoon lemon juice
- 1/2 teaspoon vanilla extract

For the raspberry sauce:

- 1 cup fresh raspberries
- 2 tablespoons granulated sugar
- 1 tablespoon water
- 1/2 teaspoon lemon juice

For serving:

- Vanilla ice cream
- Fresh raspberries
- Mint leaves (optional)

Instructions:

In a large mixing bowl, whisk together the flour, eggs, milk, melted butter, and salt until smooth. The batter should be thin and pourable. If it's too thick, you can add a bit more milk to reach the desired consistency.

Heat a non-stick skillet or crepe pan over medium heat. Add a small amount of butter or oil to the pan and swirl it around to coat the bottom evenly.

Once the pan is hot, pour about 1/4 cup of the crepe batter into the center of the pan. Quickly tilt and rotate the pan to spread the batter into a thin, even layer covering the bottom of the pan.

Cook the crepe for about 1-2 minutes, or until the edges start to lightly brown and lift away from the pan. Use a spatula to carefully flip the crepe over and cook for an additional 1-2 minutes on the other side, or until lightly golden.

Transfer the cooked crepe to a plate and set aside. Repeat with the remaining batter.

In a small saucepan, combine the sliced peaches, granulated sugar, lemon juice, and vanilla extract. Cook over medium heat, stirring occasionally, until the peaches are softened and the sugar has dissolved, about 5-7 minutes. Remove from heat and set aside.

In another small saucepan, combine the fresh raspberries, granulated sugar, water, and lemon juice. Cook over medium heat, stirring occasionally, until the raspberries break down and the sauce thickens slightly, about 5 minutes. Remove from heat and strain the sauce to remove the seeds, if desired. Set aside.

To assemble, spoon some of the peach filling onto one half of each crepe. Fold the crepe in half to cover the filling, then fold it in half again to form a triangle or roll it into a cylinder.

Place the filled crepes on serving plates. Top with a scoop of vanilla ice cream, drizzle with the raspberry sauce, and garnish with fresh raspberries and mint leaves, if desired.

Serve the Peach Melba crepes immediately and enjoy the delightful combination of tender crepes, sweet peaches, tangy raspberry sauce, and creamy vanilla ice cream—a perfect dessert for any occasion!

Pineapple Coconut Crepes

Ingredients:

For the crepes:

- 1 cup all-purpose flour
- 2 large eggs
- 1 1/4 cups coconut milk
- 2 tablespoons unsalted butter, melted
- Pinch of salt
- Butter or oil, for cooking

For the pineapple coconut filling:

- 1 cup fresh pineapple, diced
- 1/2 cup shredded coconut
- 2 tablespoons brown sugar
- 1 tablespoon unsalted butter
- 1/2 teaspoon vanilla extract

For serving:

- Additional shredded coconut for garnish
- Maple syrup or honey (optional)

Instructions:

In a large mixing bowl, whisk together the flour, eggs, coconut milk, melted butter, and salt until smooth. The batter should be thin and pourable. If it's too thick, you can add a bit more coconut milk to reach the desired consistency.

Heat a non-stick skillet or crepe pan over medium heat. Add a small amount of butter or oil to the pan and swirl it around to coat the bottom evenly.

Once the pan is hot, pour about 1/4 cup of the crepe batter into the center of the pan. Quickly tilt and rotate the pan to spread the batter into a thin, even layer covering the bottom of the pan.

Cook the crepe for about 1-2 minutes, or until the edges start to lightly brown and lift away from the pan. Use a spatula to carefully flip the crepe over and cook for an additional 1-2 minutes on the other side, or until lightly golden.

Transfer the cooked crepe to a plate and set aside. Repeat with the remaining batter.

In a skillet, melt the unsalted butter over medium heat. Add the diced pineapple and shredded coconut. Cook, stirring occasionally, until the pineapple is softened and caramelized, about 5-7 minutes.

Sprinkle the brown sugar over the pineapple and coconut mixture. Stir well to combine.

Cook for an additional 2-3 minutes, stirring occasionally, until the sugar is melted and the mixture is caramelized.

Stir in the vanilla extract and remove the skillet from heat.

Spoon a portion of the pineapple coconut filling onto one half of each crepe.

Fold the crepe in half to cover the filling, then fold it in half again to form a triangle or roll it into a cylinder.

Repeat the process with the remaining crepes and filling.

Serve the pineapple coconut crepes warm, garnished with additional shredded coconut on top. You can also drizzle with maple syrup or honey for extra sweetness if desired.

Enjoy the tropical flavors of pineapple and coconut wrapped in tender crepes—a perfect breakfast or brunch option for any day!

Mango Tango Crepes

Ingredients:

For the crepes:

- 1 cup all-purpose flour
- 2 large eggs
- 1 1/4 cups whole milk
- 2 tablespoons unsalted butter, melted
- Pinch of salt
- Butter or oil, for cooking

For the mango filling:

- 2 ripe mangoes, peeled, pitted, and thinly sliced
- 2 tablespoons granulated sugar
- 1 tablespoon fresh lime juice
- Zest of 1 lime

For the whipped cream:

- 1 cup heavy cream
- 2 tablespoons powdered sugar
- 1/2 teaspoon vanilla extract

For serving:

- Fresh mint leaves for garnish
- Additional sliced mangoes for garnish (optional)

Instructions:

In a large mixing bowl, whisk together the flour, eggs, milk, melted butter, and salt until smooth. The batter should be thin and pourable. If it's too thick, you can add a bit more milk to reach the desired consistency.

Heat a non-stick skillet or crepe pan over medium heat. Add a small amount of butter or oil to the pan and swirl it around to coat the bottom evenly.

Once the pan is hot, pour about 1/4 cup of the crepe batter into the center of the pan. Quickly tilt and rotate the pan to spread the batter into a thin, even layer covering the bottom of the pan.

Cook the crepe for about 1-2 minutes, or until the edges start to lightly brown and lift away from the pan. Use a spatula to carefully flip the crepe over and cook for an additional 1-2 minutes on the other side, or until lightly golden.

Transfer the cooked crepe to a plate and set aside. Repeat with the remaining batter.

In a bowl, toss the sliced mangoes with granulated sugar, lime juice, and lime zest until well coated.

In a separate bowl, whip the heavy cream, powdered sugar, and vanilla extract together until stiff peaks form to make whipped cream.

To assemble, place a few slices of mango in the center of each crepe.

Spoon a dollop of whipped cream over the mango slices.

Fold the crepe in half to cover the filling, then fold it in half again to form a triangle or roll it into a cylinder.

Repeat the process with the remaining crepes and filling.

Serve the mango tango crepes garnished with fresh mint leaves and additional sliced mangoes, if desired.

Enjoy the refreshing and tropical flavors of mango and lime combined with creamy whipped cream in these delightful crepes—a perfect dessert for any occasion!

Berry Blast Crepes (Assorted Berries)

Ingredients:

For the crepes:

- 1 cup all-purpose flour
- 2 large eggs
- 1 1/4 cups whole milk
- 2 tablespoons unsalted butter, melted
- Pinch of salt
- Butter or oil, for cooking

For the berry filling:

- 2 cups mixed berries (such as strawberries, blueberries, raspberries, blackberries)
- 2 tablespoons granulated sugar (adjust to taste)
- 1 tablespoon lemon juice
- Zest of 1 lemon

For serving:

- Whipped cream or vanilla ice cream
- Powdered sugar for dusting
- Fresh mint leaves for garnish (optional)

Instructions:

In a large mixing bowl, whisk together the flour, eggs, milk, melted butter, and salt until smooth. The batter should be thin and pourable. If it's too thick, you can add a bit more milk to reach the desired consistency.

Heat a non-stick skillet or crepe pan over medium heat. Add a small amount of butter or oil to the pan and swirl it around to coat the bottom evenly.

Once the pan is hot, pour about 1/4 cup of the crepe batter into the center of the pan. Quickly tilt and rotate the pan to spread the batter into a thin, even layer covering the bottom of the pan.

Cook the crepe for about 1-2 minutes, or until the edges start to lightly brown and lift away from the pan. Use a spatula to carefully flip the crepe over and cook for an additional 1-2 minutes on the other side, or until lightly golden.

Transfer the cooked crepe to a plate and set aside. Repeat with the remaining batter.

In a bowl, combine the mixed berries with granulated sugar, lemon juice, and lemon zest. Toss gently to coat the berries evenly. Adjust the amount of sugar according to your taste and the sweetness of the berries.

Spoon a generous portion of the mixed berry filling onto one half of each crepe. Fold the crepe in half to cover the filling, then fold it in half again to form a triangle or roll it into a cylinder.

Repeat the process with the remaining crepes and berry filling.

Serve the berry blast crepes warm, topped with a dollop of whipped cream or a scoop of vanilla ice cream.

Dust with powdered sugar and garnish with fresh mint leaves, if desired.

Enjoy the burst of flavors from the assorted berries in these delightful crepes—a perfect treat for breakfast, brunch, or dessert!

Tiramisu Crepes

Ingredients:

For the crepes:

- 1 cup all-purpose flour
- 2 large eggs
- 1 1/4 cups whole milk
- 2 tablespoons unsalted butter, melted
- Pinch of salt
- Butter or oil, for cooking

For the tiramisu filling:

- 8 oz (225g) mascarpone cheese, softened
- 1/2 cup powdered sugar
- 1 teaspoon vanilla extract
- 2 tablespoons coffee liqueur (such as Kahlua), optional
- 1/2 cup brewed strong coffee, cooled
- 2 tablespoons cocoa powder, for dusting

For serving:

- Chocolate shavings or grated chocolate

Instructions:

In a large mixing bowl, whisk together the flour, eggs, milk, melted butter, and salt until smooth. The batter should be thin and pourable. If it's too thick, you can add a bit more milk to reach the desired consistency.

Heat a non-stick skillet or crepe pan over medium heat. Add a small amount of butter or oil to the pan and swirl it around to coat the bottom evenly.

Once the pan is hot, pour about 1/4 cup of the crepe batter into the center of the pan. Quickly tilt and rotate the pan to spread the batter into a thin, even layer covering the bottom of the pan.

Cook the crepe for about 1-2 minutes, or until the edges start to lightly brown and lift away from the pan. Use a spatula to carefully flip the crepe over and cook for an additional 1-2 minutes on the other side, or until lightly golden.

Transfer the cooked crepe to a plate and set aside. Repeat with the remaining batter.

In a mixing bowl, beat together the mascarpone cheese, powdered sugar, vanilla extract, and coffee liqueur (if using) until smooth and creamy.

To assemble, spread a generous portion of the tiramisu filling onto one half of each crepe.

Fold the crepe in half to cover the filling, then fold it in half again to form a triangle or roll it into a cylinder.

Place the filled crepes on serving plates. Spoon a little brewed coffee over each crepe.

Dust the tiramisu crepes with cocoa powder.

Garnish with chocolate shavings or grated chocolate.

Serve the tiramisu crepes immediately, and enjoy the indulgent flavors reminiscent of the classic Italian dessert!

These tiramisu crepes make for a delightful dessert or a special treat for brunch. Enjoy!

Red Velvet Crepes

Ingredients:

For the crepes:

- 1 cup all-purpose flour
- 2 tablespoons unsweetened cocoa powder
- 2 tablespoons granulated sugar
- Pinch of salt
- 2 large eggs
- 1 1/4 cups buttermilk
- 1 tablespoon red food coloring
- 1 teaspoon vanilla extract
- 2 tablespoons unsalted butter, melted
- Butter or oil, for cooking

For the cream cheese filling:

- 8 oz (225g) cream cheese, softened
- 1/2 cup powdered sugar
- 1 teaspoon vanilla extract
- 1 cup heavy cream

For serving:

- Powdered sugar for dusting
- Fresh strawberries or raspberries for garnish (optional)

Instructions:

In a large mixing bowl, whisk together the flour, cocoa powder, granulated sugar, and salt.

In another bowl, whisk together the eggs, buttermilk, red food coloring, and vanilla extract until well combined.

Gradually add the wet ingredients to the dry ingredients, whisking continuously, until smooth and well combined.

Stir in the melted butter until fully incorporated into the batter.

Heat a non-stick skillet or crepe pan over medium heat. Add a small amount of butter or oil to the pan and swirl it around to coat the bottom evenly.

Once the pan is hot, pour about 1/4 cup of the crepe batter into the center of the pan. Quickly tilt and rotate the pan to spread the batter into a thin, even layer covering the bottom of the pan.

Cook the crepe for about 1-2 minutes, or until the edges start to lightly brown and lift away from the pan. Use a spatula to carefully flip the crepe over and cook for an additional 1-2 minutes on the other side, or until lightly golden.

Transfer the cooked crepe to a plate and set aside. Repeat with the remaining batter, stacking the cooked crepes on top of each other.

In a mixing bowl, beat the softened cream cheese, powdered sugar, and vanilla extract until smooth and creamy.

In another bowl, whip the heavy cream until stiff peaks form.

Gently fold the whipped cream into the cream cheese mixture until well combined.

To assemble, spread a generous portion of the cream cheese filling onto one half of each crepe.

Fold the crepe in half to cover the filling, then fold it in half again to form a triangle or roll it into a cylinder.

Repeat the process with the remaining crepes and filling.

Serve the red velvet crepes warm, dusted with powdered sugar and garnished with fresh strawberries or raspberries, if desired.

These red velvet crepes make for a decadent and indulgent dessert or a special treat for brunch. Enjoy!

S'mores Crepes

Ingredients:

For the crepes:

- 1 cup all-purpose flour
- 2 large eggs
- 1 1/4 cups whole milk
- 2 tablespoons unsalted butter, melted
- Pinch of salt
- Butter or oil, for cooking

For the s'mores filling:

- 1 cup mini marshmallows
- 1 cup chocolate chips or chopped chocolate
- 1/2 cup graham cracker crumbs

For serving:

- Additional graham cracker crumbs for garnish
- Chocolate sauce (optional)
- Marshmallow fluff (optional)

Instructions:

In a large mixing bowl, whisk together the flour, eggs, milk, melted butter, and salt until smooth. The batter should be thin and pourable. If it's too thick, you can add a bit more milk to reach the desired consistency.

Heat a non-stick skillet or crepe pan over medium heat. Add a small amount of butter or oil to the pan and swirl it around to coat the bottom evenly.

Once the pan is hot, pour about 1/4 cup of the crepe batter into the center of the pan. Quickly tilt and rotate the pan to spread the batter into a thin, even layer covering the bottom of the pan.

Cook the crepe for about 1-2 minutes, or until the edges start to lightly brown and lift away from the pan. Use a spatula to carefully flip the crepe over and cook for an additional 1-2 minutes on the other side, or until lightly golden.

Transfer the cooked crepe to a plate and set aside. Repeat with the remaining batter.

Sprinkle a handful of mini marshmallows, chocolate chips, and graham cracker crumbs onto one half of each crepe.

Fold the crepe in half to cover the filling, then fold it in half again to form a triangle or roll it into a cylinder.

Repeat the process with the remaining crepes and filling.

To serve, sprinkle additional graham cracker crumbs over the top of the crepes. Drizzle with chocolate sauce and marshmallow fluff, if desired.

Serve the s'mores crepes warm and enjoy the delicious combination of melted chocolate, gooey marshmallows, and crunchy graham crackers wrapped in tender crepes—a perfect treat for dessert or a special breakfast!

Pumpkin Spice Crepes

Ingredients:

For the crepes:

- 1 cup all-purpose flour
- 2 large eggs
- 1 cup milk
- 1/2 cup pumpkin puree
- 2 tablespoons unsalted butter, melted
- 2 tablespoons granulated sugar
- 1 teaspoon pumpkin pie spice
- Pinch of salt
- Butter or oil, for cooking

For the filling:

- 1 cup whipped cream or whipped topping
- Maple syrup or caramel sauce, for drizzling (optional)
- Chopped pecans or walnuts, for garnish (optional)

Instructions:

In a large mixing bowl, whisk together the flour, eggs, milk, pumpkin puree, melted butter, sugar, pumpkin pie spice, and salt until smooth. The batter should be thin and pourable. If it's too thick, you can add a bit more milk to reach the desired consistency.

Heat a non-stick skillet or crepe pan over medium heat. Add a small amount of butter or oil to the pan and swirl it around to coat the bottom evenly.

Once the pan is hot, pour about 1/4 cup of the crepe batter into the center of the pan. Quickly tilt and rotate the pan to spread the batter into a thin, even layer covering the bottom of the pan.

Cook the crepe for about 1-2 minutes, or until the edges start to lightly brown and lift away from the pan. Use a spatula to carefully flip the crepe over and cook for an additional 1-2 minutes on the other side, or until lightly golden.

Transfer the cooked crepe to a plate and set aside. Repeat with the remaining batter.

To assemble, spread a generous portion of whipped cream or whipped topping onto one half of each crepe.

Fold the crepe in half to cover the filling, then fold it in half again to form a triangle or roll it into a cylinder.

Repeat the process with the remaining crepes and whipped cream.

Drizzle with maple syrup or caramel sauce, if desired.

Garnish with chopped pecans or walnuts, if using.

Serve the pumpkin spice crepes warm and enjoy the delightful flavors of pumpkin, spices, and whipped cream—a perfect fall-inspired treat for breakfast or dessert!

Cinnamon Roll Crepes

Ingredients:

For the crepes:

- 1 cup all-purpose flour
- 2 large eggs
- 1 1/4 cups whole milk
- 2 tablespoons unsalted butter, melted
- Pinch of salt
- Butter or oil, for cooking

For the cinnamon filling:

- 1/4 cup unsalted butter, softened
- 1/2 cup brown sugar
- 1 tablespoon ground cinnamon

For the cream cheese glaze:

- 4 oz (115g) cream cheese, softened
- 1/4 cup unsalted butter, softened
- 1 cup powdered sugar
- 1/2 teaspoon vanilla extract
- 2-3 tablespoons milk

Instructions:

In a large mixing bowl, whisk together the flour, eggs, milk, melted butter, and salt until smooth. The batter should be thin and pourable. If it's too thick, you can add a bit more milk to reach the desired consistency.

Heat a non-stick skillet or crepe pan over medium heat. Add a small amount of butter or oil to the pan and swirl it around to coat the bottom evenly.

Once the pan is hot, pour about 1/4 cup of the crepe batter into the center of the pan. Quickly tilt and rotate the pan to spread the batter into a thin, even layer covering the bottom of the pan.

Cook the crepe for about 1-2 minutes, or until the edges start to lightly brown and lift away from the pan. Use a spatula to carefully flip the crepe over and cook for an additional 1-2 minutes on the other side, or until lightly golden.

Transfer the cooked crepe to a plate and set aside. Repeat with the remaining batter.

In a small bowl, mix together the softened butter, brown sugar, and ground cinnamon until well combined to make the cinnamon filling.

Spread a thin layer of the cinnamon filling onto each crepe.

Roll up each crepe into a tight spiral.

In another bowl, beat together the softened cream cheese, softened butter, powdered sugar, and vanilla extract until smooth to make the cream cheese glaze.

Gradually add milk to the cream cheese mixture, 1 tablespoon at a time, until you reach your desired consistency for the glaze.

Drizzle the cream cheese glaze over the rolled-up crepes.

Serve the cinnamon roll crepes warm and enjoy the delightful flavors of cinnamon, sugar, and cream cheese—a perfect treat for breakfast or brunch!

Pecan Pie Crepes

Ingredients:

For the crepes:

- 1 cup all-purpose flour
- 2 large eggs
- 1 1/4 cups whole milk
- 2 tablespoons unsalted butter, melted
- Pinch of salt
- Butter or oil, for cooking

For the pecan pie filling:

- 1 cup chopped pecans
- 1/2 cup packed brown sugar
- 1/4 cup corn syrup
- 2 tablespoons unsalted butter
- 1 teaspoon vanilla extract
- Pinch of salt

For serving:

- Whipped cream or vanilla ice cream
- Additional chopped pecans for garnish
- Maple syrup or caramel sauce (optional)

Instructions:

In a large mixing bowl, whisk together the flour, eggs, milk, melted butter, and salt until smooth. The batter should be thin and pourable. If it's too thick, you can add a bit more milk to reach the desired consistency.

Heat a non-stick skillet or crepe pan over medium heat. Add a small amount of butter or oil to the pan and swirl it around to coat the bottom evenly.

Once the pan is hot, pour about 1/4 cup of the crepe batter into the center of the pan. Quickly tilt and rotate the pan to spread the batter into a thin, even layer covering the bottom of the pan.

Cook the crepe for about 1-2 minutes, or until the edges start to lightly brown and lift away from the pan. Use a spatula to carefully flip the crepe over and cook for an additional 1-2 minutes on the other side, or until lightly golden.

Transfer the cooked crepe to a plate and set aside. Repeat with the remaining batter.

In a saucepan, combine the chopped pecans, brown sugar, corn syrup, unsalted butter, vanilla extract, and a pinch of salt. Cook over medium heat, stirring constantly, until the mixture is bubbly and the sugar has dissolved, about 3-4 minutes. Remove from heat.

Spoon a generous portion of the pecan pie filling onto one half of each crepe. Fold the crepe in half to cover the filling, then fold it in half again to form a triangle or roll it into a cylinder.

Repeat the process with the remaining crepes and filling.

Serve the pecan pie crepes warm, topped with whipped cream or a scoop of vanilla ice cream.

Garnish with additional chopped pecans and drizzle with maple syrup or caramel sauce, if desired.

Enjoy the delicious combination of tender crepes filled with sweet and nutty pecan pie filling—a perfect dessert for any occasion!

Maple Bacon Crepes

Ingredients:

For the crepes:

- 1 cup all-purpose flour
- 2 large eggs
- 1 1/4 cups whole milk
- 2 tablespoons unsalted butter, melted
- Pinch of salt
- Butter or oil, for cooking

For the maple bacon filling:

- 8 slices bacon
- 1/4 cup maple syrup
- 2 tablespoons brown sugar
- 1/2 teaspoon ground cinnamon (optional)

For serving:

- Maple syrup for drizzling
- Powdered sugar (optional)
- Fresh berries for garnish (optional)

Instructions:

Cook the bacon slices in a skillet over medium heat until crispy. Remove from the skillet and place them on paper towels to drain excess grease. Once cooled, chop the bacon into small pieces.

In a small bowl, mix together the maple syrup, brown sugar, and ground cinnamon (if using). Add the chopped bacon to the mixture and stir until well coated.

In a separate bowl, prepare the crepe batter by whisking together the flour, eggs, milk, melted butter, and pinch of salt until smooth.

Heat a non-stick skillet or crepe pan over medium heat. Add a small amount of butter or oil to the pan and swirl it around to coat the bottom evenly.

Once the pan is hot, pour about 1/4 cup of the crepe batter into the center of the pan. Quickly tilt and rotate the pan to spread the batter into a thin, even layer covering the bottom of the pan.

Cook the crepe for about 1-2 minutes, or until the edges start to lightly brown and lift away from the pan. Use a spatula to carefully flip the crepe over and cook for an additional 1-2 minutes on the other side, or until lightly golden.

Transfer the cooked crepe to a plate and set aside. Repeat with the remaining batter.

Once all the crepes are cooked, spoon a portion of the maple bacon mixture onto one half of each crepe.

Fold the crepe in half to cover the filling, then fold it in half again to form a triangle or roll it into a cylinder.

Repeat the process with the remaining crepes and filling.

Serve the maple bacon crepes warm, drizzled with additional maple syrup and powdered sugar if desired.

Garnish with fresh berries for a pop of color and freshness, if desired.

Enjoy the sweet and savory combination of maple syrup and crispy bacon wrapped in tender crepes—a delicious breakfast or brunch option!

Irish Cream Crepes

Ingredients:

For the crepes:

- 1 cup all-purpose flour
- 2 large eggs
- 1 1/4 cups whole milk
- 2 tablespoons unsalted butter, melted
- Pinch of salt
- Butter or oil, for cooking

For the Irish cream filling:

- 1/2 cup heavy cream
- 1/4 cup Irish cream liqueur (such as Baileys)
- 2 tablespoons powdered sugar
- 1/2 teaspoon vanilla extract
- Zest of 1 orange (optional)

For serving:

- Chocolate sauce (optional)
- Whipped cream (optional)
- Fresh berries (optional)

Instructions:

In a large mixing bowl, whisk together the flour, eggs, milk, melted butter, and salt until smooth. The batter should be thin and pourable. If it's too thick, you can add a bit more milk to reach the desired consistency.
Heat a non-stick skillet or crepe pan over medium heat. Add a small amount of butter or oil to the pan and swirl it around to coat the bottom evenly.
Once the pan is hot, pour about 1/4 cup of the crepe batter into the center of the pan. Quickly tilt and rotate the pan to spread the batter into a thin, even layer covering the bottom of the pan.
Cook the crepe for about 1-2 minutes, or until the edges start to lightly brown and lift away from the pan. Use a spatula to carefully flip the crepe over and cook for an additional 1-2 minutes on the other side, or until lightly golden.

Transfer the cooked crepe to a plate and set aside. Repeat with the remaining batter.

In a mixing bowl, whip the heavy cream until soft peaks form.

Fold in the Irish cream liqueur, powdered sugar, vanilla extract, and orange zest (if using) until well combined.

Spoon a generous portion of the Irish cream filling onto one half of each crepe.

Fold the crepe in half to cover the filling, then fold it in half again to form a triangle or roll it into a cylinder.

Repeat the process with the remaining crepes and filling.

Serve the Irish cream crepes warm, drizzled with chocolate sauce and topped with whipped cream and fresh berries if desired.

Enjoy the rich and creamy flavor of Irish cream liqueur wrapped in tender crepes—a perfect treat for brunch or dessert!

Lemon Meringue Crepes

Ingredients:

For the crepes:

- 1 cup all-purpose flour
- 2 large eggs
- 1 1/4 cups whole milk
- 2 tablespoons unsalted butter, melted
- Pinch of salt
- Butter or oil, for cooking

For the lemon curd filling:

- 3 large eggs
- 3/4 cup granulated sugar
- 1/2 cup freshly squeezed lemon juice
- Zest of 2 lemons
- 6 tablespoons unsalted butter, cubed

For the meringue topping:

- 3 large egg whites
- 1/4 teaspoon cream of tartar
- 6 tablespoons granulated sugar

Instructions:

In a large mixing bowl, whisk together the flour, eggs, milk, melted butter, and salt until smooth. The batter should be thin and pourable. If it's too thick, you can add a bit more milk to reach the desired consistency.

Heat a non-stick skillet or crepe pan over medium heat. Add a small amount of butter or oil to the pan and swirl it around to coat the bottom evenly.

Once the pan is hot, pour about 1/4 cup of the crepe batter into the center of the pan. Quickly tilt and rotate the pan to spread the batter into a thin, even layer covering the bottom of the pan.

Cook the crepe for about 1-2 minutes, or until the edges start to lightly brown and lift away from the pan. Use a spatula to carefully flip the crepe over and cook for an additional 1-2 minutes on the other side, or until lightly golden.

Transfer the cooked crepe to a plate and set aside. Repeat with the remaining batter.

In a heatproof bowl, whisk together the eggs, granulated sugar, lemon juice, and lemon zest.

Place the bowl over a saucepan of simmering water (double boiler) and cook, stirring constantly, until the mixture thickens and coats the back of a spoon, about 8-10 minutes.

Remove the bowl from heat and whisk in the cubed butter until melted and smooth. Allow the lemon curd to cool slightly.

Spread a generous portion of lemon curd onto one half of each crepe.

To make the meringue topping, in a clean mixing bowl, beat the egg whites and cream of tartar on medium speed until soft peaks form.

Gradually add the granulated sugar, 1 tablespoon at a time, while continuing to beat on high speed until stiff peaks form and the sugar is dissolved.

Spoon or pipe the meringue over the lemon curd-filled half of each crepe.

Using a kitchen torch or placing under a preheated broiler, lightly brown the meringue until golden and toasted.

Serve the lemon meringue crepes warm and enjoy the delightful combination of tangy lemon curd and fluffy meringue atop tender crepes—a perfect dessert for any occasion!

Black Forest Crepes (Cherry, Chocolate)

Ingredients:

For the crepes:

- 1 cup all-purpose flour
- 2 large eggs
- 1 1/4 cups whole milk
- 2 tablespoons unsalted butter, melted
- 2 tablespoons granulated sugar
- 2 tablespoons cocoa powder
- Pinch of salt
- Butter or oil, for cooking

For the cherry filling:

- 2 cups pitted cherries (fresh or frozen)
- 1/4 cup granulated sugar
- 1 tablespoon cornstarch
- 1/4 cup water
- 1 teaspoon lemon juice
- 1/2 teaspoon vanilla extract

For serving:

- Whipped cream
- Chocolate shavings or grated chocolate
- Additional cherries for garnish (optional)
- Powdered sugar for dusting (optional)

Instructions:

In a large mixing bowl, whisk together the flour, eggs, milk, melted butter, sugar, cocoa powder, and salt until smooth. The batter should be thin and pourable. If it's too thick, you can add a bit more milk to reach the desired consistency. Heat a non-stick skillet or crepe pan over medium heat. Add a small amount of butter or oil to the pan and swirl it around to coat the bottom evenly.

Once the pan is hot, pour about 1/4 cup of the crepe batter into the center of the pan. Quickly tilt and rotate the pan to spread the batter into a thin, even layer covering the bottom of the pan.

Cook the crepe for about 1-2 minutes, or until the edges start to lightly brown and lift away from the pan. Use a spatula to carefully flip the crepe over and cook for an additional 1-2 minutes on the other side, or until lightly golden.

Transfer the cooked crepe to a plate and set aside. Repeat with the remaining batter.

In a saucepan, combine the pitted cherries, granulated sugar, cornstarch, water, lemon juice, and vanilla extract. Cook over medium heat, stirring occasionally, until the cherries are soft and the mixture has thickened, about 5-7 minutes. Remove from heat and let it cool slightly.

To assemble, spoon a portion of the cherry filling onto one half of each crepe. Fold the crepe in half to cover the filling, then fold it in half again to form a triangle or roll it into a cylinder.

Repeat the process with the remaining crepes and cherry filling.

Serve the Black Forest crepes warm, topped with whipped cream, chocolate shavings, and additional cherries if desired.

Dust with powdered sugar for an extra touch of sweetness, if desired.

Enjoy the decadent combination of cherries and chocolate wrapped in tender crepes—a delightful dessert inspired by the classic Black Forest cake!

Cannoli Crepes

Ingredients:

For the crepes:

- 1 cup all-purpose flour
- 2 large eggs
- 1 1/4 cups whole milk
- 2 tablespoons unsalted butter, melted
- 2 tablespoons granulated sugar
- 1/2 teaspoon vanilla extract
- Pinch of salt
- Butter or oil, for cooking

For the cannoli filling:

- 1 cup ricotta cheese
- 1/4 cup powdered sugar
- 1/2 teaspoon vanilla extract
- 1/4 cup mini chocolate chips
- Zest of 1 orange (optional)

For serving:

- Powdered sugar for dusting
- Additional mini chocolate chips for garnish
- Orange zest for garnish (optional)
- Cannoli shells, broken into pieces (optional)

Instructions:

In a large mixing bowl, whisk together the flour, eggs, milk, melted butter, sugar, vanilla extract, and salt until smooth. The batter should be thin and pourable. If it's too thick, you can add a bit more milk to reach the desired consistency.
Heat a non-stick skillet or crepe pan over medium heat. Add a small amount of butter or oil to the pan and swirl it around to coat the bottom evenly.
Once the pan is hot, pour about 1/4 cup of the crepe batter into the center of the pan. Quickly tilt and rotate the pan to spread the batter into a thin, even layer covering the bottom of the pan.

Cook the crepe for about 1-2 minutes, or until the edges start to lightly brown and lift away from the pan. Use a spatula to carefully flip the crepe over and cook for an additional 1-2 minutes on the other side, or until lightly golden.

Transfer the cooked crepe to a plate and set aside. Repeat with the remaining batter.

In a mixing bowl, combine the ricotta cheese, powdered sugar, vanilla extract, mini chocolate chips, and orange zest (if using). Mix until well combined.

Spread a generous portion of the cannoli filling onto one half of each crepe.

Fold the crepe in half to cover the filling, then fold it in half again to form a triangle or roll it into a cylinder.

Repeat the process with the remaining crepes and filling.

Serve the cannoli crepes warm, dusted with powdered sugar and garnished with additional mini chocolate chips and orange zest if desired.

For an extra touch of authenticity, you can also sprinkle broken pieces of cannoli shells over the crepes before serving.

Enjoy the delicious flavors of cannoli wrapped in tender crepes—a delightful Italian-inspired dessert!

Key Lime Pie Crepes

Ingredients:

For the crepes:

- 1 cup all-purpose flour
- 2 large eggs
- 1 1/4 cups whole milk
- 2 tablespoons unsalted butter, melted
- 2 tablespoons granulated sugar
- 1/2 teaspoon vanilla extract
- Pinch of salt
- Butter or oil, for cooking

For the key lime filling:

- 1/2 cup key lime juice (freshly squeezed if possible)
- Zest of 2-3 limes
- 1/2 cup sweetened condensed milk
- 1/4 cup heavy cream
- 2 tablespoons granulated sugar (optional, adjust to taste)

For serving:

- Whipped cream
- Additional lime zest for garnish
- Graham cracker crumbs for garnish

Instructions:

In a large mixing bowl, whisk together the flour, eggs, milk, melted butter, sugar, vanilla extract, and salt until smooth. The batter should be thin and pourable. If it's too thick, you can add a bit more milk to reach the desired consistency. Heat a non-stick skillet or crepe pan over medium heat. Add a small amount of butter or oil to the pan and swirl it around to coat the bottom evenly.

Once the pan is hot, pour about 1/4 cup of the crepe batter into the center of the pan. Quickly tilt and rotate the pan to spread the batter into a thin, even layer covering the bottom of the pan.

Cook the crepe for about 1-2 minutes, or until the edges start to lightly brown and lift away from the pan. Use a spatula to carefully flip the crepe over and cook for an additional 1-2 minutes on the other side, or until lightly golden.

Transfer the cooked crepe to a plate and set aside. Repeat with the remaining batter.

In a mixing bowl, combine the key lime juice, lime zest, sweetened condensed milk, heavy cream, and granulated sugar (if using). Mix until well combined and smooth.

Spoon a generous portion of the key lime filling onto one half of each crepe.

Fold the crepe in half to cover the filling, then fold it in half again to form a triangle or roll it into a cylinder.

Repeat the process with the remaining crepes and filling.

Serve the key lime pie crepes warm, topped with whipped cream, additional lime zest, and graham cracker crumbs for garnish.

Enjoy the refreshing and tangy flavor of key lime pie wrapped in tender crepes—a delightful dessert perfect for any occasion!

Chocolate Peanut Butter Cup Crepes

Ingredients:

For the crepes:

- 1 cup all-purpose flour
- 2 large eggs
- 1 1/4 cups whole milk
- 2 tablespoons unsalted butter, melted
- 2 tablespoons cocoa powder
- 2 tablespoons granulated sugar
- Pinch of salt
- Butter or oil, for cooking

For the peanut butter filling:

- 1/2 cup creamy peanut butter
- 2 tablespoons powdered sugar
- 1/2 teaspoon vanilla extract
- 2-3 tablespoons milk

For serving:

- Chocolate sauce
- Whipped cream
- Chopped peanuts (optional)
- Mini peanut butter cups, chopped (optional)

Instructions:

In a large mixing bowl, whisk together the flour, eggs, milk, melted butter, cocoa powder, sugar, and salt until smooth. The batter should be thin and pourable. If it's too thick, you can add a bit more milk to reach the desired consistency. Heat a non-stick skillet or crepe pan over medium heat. Add a small amount of butter or oil to the pan and swirl it around to coat the bottom evenly.

Once the pan is hot, pour about 1/4 cup of the crepe batter into the center of the pan. Quickly tilt and rotate the pan to spread the batter into a thin, even layer covering the bottom of the pan.

Cook the crepe for about 1-2 minutes, or until the edges start to lightly brown and lift away from the pan. Use a spatula to carefully flip the crepe over and cook for an additional 1-2 minutes on the other side, or until lightly golden.

Transfer the cooked crepe to a plate and set aside. Repeat with the remaining batter.

In a mixing bowl, combine the creamy peanut butter, powdered sugar, vanilla extract, and milk. Mix until smooth and creamy, adding more milk as needed to reach your desired consistency for the filling.

Spread a generous portion of the peanut butter filling onto one half of each crepe.

Fold the crepe in half to cover the filling, then fold it in half again to form a triangle or roll it into a cylinder.

Repeat the process with the remaining crepes and peanut butter filling.

To serve, drizzle the chocolate sauce over the stuffed crepes and top with whipped cream.

Sprinkle with chopped peanuts and mini peanut butter cups for extra indulgence, if desired.

Enjoy the delicious combination of chocolate and peanut butter wrapped in tender crepes—a perfect dessert for peanut butter cup lovers!

Bananas Foster Crepes

Ingredients:

For the crepes:

- 1 cup all-purpose flour
- 2 large eggs
- 1 1/4 cups whole milk
- 2 tablespoons unsalted butter, melted
- 2 tablespoons granulated sugar
- 1/2 teaspoon vanilla extract
- Pinch of salt
- Butter or oil, for cooking

For the bananas foster filling:

- 3 ripe bananas, sliced
- 1/4 cup unsalted butter
- 1/2 cup brown sugar
- 1/4 cup dark rum
- 1 teaspoon ground cinnamon (optional)
- Pinch of nutmeg (optional)
- Vanilla ice cream (for serving)

Instructions:

In a large mixing bowl, whisk together the flour, eggs, milk, melted butter, sugar, vanilla extract, and salt until smooth. The batter should be thin and pourable. If it's too thick, you can add a bit more milk to reach the desired consistency.

Heat a non-stick skillet or crepe pan over medium heat. Add a small amount of butter or oil to the pan and swirl it around to coat the bottom evenly.

Once the pan is hot, pour about 1/4 cup of the crepe batter into the center of the pan. Quickly tilt and rotate the pan to spread the batter into a thin, even layer covering the bottom of the pan.

Cook the crepe for about 1-2 minutes, or until the edges start to lightly brown and lift away from the pan. Use a spatula to carefully flip the crepe over and cook for an additional 1-2 minutes on the other side, or until lightly golden.

Transfer the cooked crepe to a plate and set aside. Repeat with the remaining batter.

In a large skillet or frying pan, melt the unsalted butter over medium heat. Add the brown sugar and stir until it's dissolved and bubbling.

Add the sliced bananas to the skillet and cook for 2-3 minutes, stirring gently, until they start to soften.

Carefully pour in the dark rum and allow it to simmer for another 2-3 minutes, stirring occasionally, until the sauce thickens slightly and the alcohol cooks off.

Add ground cinnamon and nutmeg if desired.

Spoon a portion of the bananas foster filling onto one half of each crepe.

Fold the crepe in half to cover the filling, then fold it in half again to form a triangle or roll it into a cylinder.

Repeat the process with the remaining crepes and bananas foster filling.

Serve the bananas foster crepes warm, topped with a scoop of vanilla ice cream.

Enjoy the delicious flavors of caramelized bananas and rum sauce wrapped in tender crepes—a delightful dessert with a hint of indulgence!

Strawberry Shortcake Crepes

Ingredients:

For the crepes:

- 1 cup all-purpose flour
- 2 large eggs
- 1 1/4 cups whole milk
- 2 tablespoons unsalted butter, melted
- 2 tablespoons granulated sugar
- 1/2 teaspoon vanilla extract
- Pinch of salt
- Butter or oil, for cooking

For the strawberry filling:

- 2 cups fresh strawberries, hulled and sliced
- 2 tablespoons granulated sugar
- 1 tablespoon lemon juice

For the whipped cream:

- 1 cup heavy cream
- 2 tablespoons powdered sugar
- 1/2 teaspoon vanilla extract

For serving:

- Additional sliced strawberries
- Powdered sugar for dusting

Instructions:

In a large mixing bowl, whisk together the flour, eggs, milk, melted butter, sugar, vanilla extract, and salt until smooth. The batter should be thin and pourable. If it's too thick, you can add a bit more milk to reach the desired consistency.

Heat a non-stick skillet or crepe pan over medium heat. Add a small amount of butter or oil to the pan and swirl it around to coat the bottom evenly.

Once the pan is hot, pour about 1/4 cup of the crepe batter into the center of the pan. Quickly tilt and rotate the pan to spread the batter into a thin, even layer covering the bottom of the pan.

Cook the crepe for about 1-2 minutes, or until the edges start to lightly brown and lift away from the pan. Use a spatula to carefully flip the crepe over and cook for an additional 1-2 minutes on the other side, or until lightly golden.

Transfer the cooked crepe to a plate and set aside. Repeat with the remaining batter.

In a mixing bowl, combine the sliced strawberries, granulated sugar, and lemon juice. Stir until the strawberries are well coated, then set aside to macerate for 10-15 minutes.

In another mixing bowl, whip the heavy cream until it begins to thicken. Add the powdered sugar and vanilla extract, then continue to whip until soft peaks form.

To assemble, spoon a portion of the macerated strawberries onto one half of each crepe.

Top the strawberries with a dollop of whipped cream.

Fold the crepe in half to cover the filling, then fold it in half again to form a triangle or roll it into a cylinder.

Repeat the process with the remaining crepes and filling.

Serve the strawberry shortcake crepes warm, topped with additional sliced strawberries and a dusting of powdered sugar.

Enjoy the delightful combination of sweet strawberries, fluffy whipped cream, and tender crepes—a perfect dessert for any occasion!

Salted Caramel Pretzel Crepes

Ingredients:

For the crepes:

- 1 cup all-purpose flour
- 2 large eggs
- 1 1/4 cups whole milk
- 2 tablespoons unsalted butter, melted
- 2 tablespoons granulated sugar
- Pinch of salt
- Butter or oil, for cooking

For the salted caramel sauce:

- 1 cup granulated sugar
- 6 tablespoons unsalted butter, cubed
- 1/2 cup heavy cream
- 1 teaspoon sea salt flakes

For the pretzel topping:

- 1 cup pretzels, crushed into small pieces

For serving:

- Whipped cream or vanilla ice cream (optional)

Instructions:

In a large mixing bowl, whisk together the flour, eggs, milk, melted butter, sugar, and salt until smooth. The batter should be thin and pourable. If it's too thick, you can add a bit more milk to reach the desired consistency.

Heat a non-stick skillet or crepe pan over medium heat. Add a small amount of butter or oil to the pan and swirl it around to coat the bottom evenly.

Once the pan is hot, pour about 1/4 cup of the crepe batter into the center of the pan. Quickly tilt and rotate the pan to spread the batter into a thin, even layer covering the bottom of the pan.

Cook the crepe for about 1-2 minutes, or until the edges start to lightly brown and lift away from the pan. Use a spatula to carefully flip the crepe over and cook for an additional 1-2 minutes on the other side, or until lightly golden.

Transfer the cooked crepe to a plate and set aside. Repeat with the remaining batter.

To make the salted caramel sauce, heat granulated sugar in a saucepan over medium heat, stirring constantly with a rubber spatula. Sugar will form clumps and eventually melt into a thick brown, amber-colored liquid as you continue to stir.

Once the sugar is completely melted, add the butter. The caramel will bubble rapidly when you add the butter, so be careful.

Stir the butter into the caramel until it is completely melted, about 2-3 minutes. Slowly drizzle in the heavy cream while stirring. Allow the mixture to boil for 1 minute. It will rise in the pan as it boils.

Remove from heat and stir in the sea salt. Allow to cool slightly.

Spread a generous amount of salted caramel sauce onto each crepe.

Sprinkle crushed pretzel pieces over the caramel sauce.

Fold the crepe in half to cover the filling, then fold it in half again to form a triangle or roll it into a cylinder.

Repeat the process with the remaining crepes and filling.

Serve the salted caramel pretzel crepes warm, optionally topped with whipped cream or vanilla ice cream.

Enjoy the delightful combination of sweet and salty flavors wrapped in tender crepes—a perfect treat for any occasion!

Mint Chocolate Chip Crepes

Ingredients:

For the crepes:

- 1 cup all-purpose flour
- 2 large eggs
- 1 1/4 cups whole milk
- 2 tablespoons unsalted butter, melted
- 2 tablespoons granulated sugar
- 2 tablespoons cocoa powder
- 1/2 teaspoon mint extract
- Pinch of salt
- Butter or oil, for cooking

For the mint chocolate chip filling:

- 1 cup heavy cream
- 2 tablespoons powdered sugar
- 1/2 teaspoon mint extract
- 1/2 cup mini chocolate chips
- Green food coloring (optional)

For serving:

- Additional mini chocolate chips
- Fresh mint leaves (optional)
- Whipped cream (optional)

Instructions:

In a large mixing bowl, whisk together the flour, eggs, milk, melted butter, sugar, cocoa powder, mint extract, and salt until smooth. The batter should be thin and pourable. If it's too thick, you can add a bit more milk to reach the desired consistency.
Heat a non-stick skillet or crepe pan over medium heat. Add a small amount of butter or oil to the pan and swirl it around to coat the bottom evenly.

Once the pan is hot, pour about 1/4 cup of the crepe batter into the center of the pan. Quickly tilt and rotate the pan to spread the batter into a thin, even layer covering the bottom of the pan.

Cook the crepe for about 1-2 minutes, or until the edges start to lightly brown and lift away from the pan. Use a spatula to carefully flip the crepe over and cook for an additional 1-2 minutes on the other side, or until lightly golden.

Transfer the cooked crepe to a plate and set aside. Repeat with the remaining batter.

In a mixing bowl, whip the heavy cream until it begins to thicken. Add the powdered sugar and mint extract, then continue to whip until soft peaks form.

Fold in the mini chocolate chips and green food coloring (if using) until evenly distributed.

Spoon a portion of the mint chocolate chip filling onto one half of each crepe. Fold the crepe in half to cover the filling, then fold it in half again to form a triangle or roll it into a cylinder.

Repeat the process with the remaining crepes and filling.

Serve the mint chocolate chip crepes warm, topped with additional mini chocolate chips and fresh mint leaves if desired.

Optionally, serve with a dollop of whipped cream on top.

Enjoy the refreshing flavor of mint paired with rich chocolate wrapped in tender crepes—a delightful dessert for any mint chocolate lover!

Raspberry White Chocolate Crepes

Ingredients:

For the crepes:

- 1 cup all-purpose flour
- 2 large eggs
- 1 1/4 cups whole milk
- 2 tablespoons unsalted butter, melted
- 2 tablespoons granulated sugar
- Pinch of salt
- Butter or oil, for cooking

For the white chocolate filling:

- 1 cup white chocolate chips
- 1/2 cup heavy cream
- 1 teaspoon vanilla extract

For the raspberry sauce:

- 1 cup fresh raspberries
- 2 tablespoons granulated sugar
- 1 tablespoon water
- 1/2 teaspoon lemon juice

For serving:

- Fresh raspberries
- Powdered sugar for dusting
- White chocolate shavings or curls (optional)

Instructions:

In a large mixing bowl, whisk together the flour, eggs, milk, melted butter, sugar, and salt until smooth. The batter should be thin and pourable. If it's too thick, you can add a bit more milk to reach the desired consistency.

Heat a non-stick skillet or crepe pan over medium heat. Add a small amount of butter or oil to the pan and swirl it around to coat the bottom evenly.

Once the pan is hot, pour about 1/4 cup of the crepe batter into the center of the pan. Quickly tilt and rotate the pan to spread the batter into a thin, even layer covering the bottom of the pan.

Cook the crepe for about 1-2 minutes, or until the edges start to lightly brown and lift away from the pan. Use a spatula to carefully flip the crepe over and cook for an additional 1-2 minutes on the other side, or until lightly golden.

Transfer the cooked crepe to a plate and set aside. Repeat with the remaining batter.

In a small saucepan, heat the heavy cream over medium-low heat until it just begins to simmer. Remove from heat and add the white chocolate chips. Let sit for 1-2 minutes, then stir until the chocolate is melted and the mixture is smooth. Stir in the vanilla extract. Keep warm.

In another saucepan, combine the raspberries, granulated sugar, water, and lemon juice. Cook over medium heat, stirring occasionally, until the raspberries break down and the mixture thickens slightly, about 5-7 minutes. Remove from heat and strain the mixture through a fine mesh sieve to remove the seeds. Allow to cool slightly.

To assemble, spoon a portion of the white chocolate filling onto one half of each crepe.

Spoon some of the raspberry sauce over the white chocolate filling.

Fold the crepe in half to cover the filling, then fold it in half again to form a triangle or roll it into a cylinder.

Repeat the process with the remaining crepes and filling.

Serve the raspberry white chocolate crepes warm, topped with fresh raspberries, a dusting of powdered sugar, and white chocolate shavings or curls if desired.

Enjoy the irresistible combination of sweet white chocolate and tart raspberries wrapped in tender crepes—a perfect dessert for any occasion!

Lemon Blueberry Mascarpone Crepes

Ingredients:

For the crepes:

- 1 cup all-purpose flour
- 2 large eggs
- 1 1/4 cups whole milk
- 2 tablespoons unsalted butter, melted
- 2 tablespoons granulated sugar
- Zest of 1 lemon
- 1/2 teaspoon vanilla extract
- Pinch of salt
- Butter or oil, for cooking

For the blueberry compote:

- 2 cups fresh or frozen blueberries
- 1/4 cup granulated sugar
- 2 tablespoons water
- Zest and juice of 1 lemon
- 1 teaspoon cornstarch mixed with 1 tablespoon water (optional, for thickening)

For the mascarpone filling:

- 1 cup mascarpone cheese
- 2 tablespoons powdered sugar
- 1 teaspoon vanilla extract
- Zest of 1 lemon

For serving:

- Fresh blueberries
- Powdered sugar for dusting
- Lemon zest for garnish

Instructions:

In a large mixing bowl, whisk together the flour, eggs, milk, melted butter, sugar, lemon zest, vanilla extract, and salt until smooth. The batter should be thin and pourable. If it's too thick, you can add a bit more milk to reach the desired consistency.

Heat a non-stick skillet or crepe pan over medium heat. Add a small amount of butter or oil to the pan and swirl it around to coat the bottom evenly.

Once the pan is hot, pour about 1/4 cup of the crepe batter into the center of the pan. Quickly tilt and rotate the pan to spread the batter into a thin, even layer covering the bottom of the pan.

Cook the crepe for about 1-2 minutes, or until the edges start to lightly brown and lift away from the pan. Use a spatula to carefully flip the crepe over and cook for an additional 1-2 minutes on the other side, or until lightly golden.

Transfer the cooked crepe to a plate and set aside. Repeat with the remaining batter.

In a saucepan, combine the blueberries, granulated sugar, water, lemon zest, and lemon juice. Cook over medium heat, stirring occasionally, until the blueberries burst and release their juices, about 5-7 minutes.

If desired, mix the cornstarch with water to create a slurry, then stir it into the blueberry mixture to thicken the compote slightly. Cook for an additional 1-2 minutes, then remove from heat and let it cool slightly.

In a mixing bowl, combine the mascarpone cheese, powdered sugar, vanilla extract, and lemon zest. Mix until smooth and well combined.

To assemble, spread a generous portion of the mascarpone filling onto one half of each crepe.

Spoon some of the blueberry compote over the mascarpone filling.

Fold the crepe in half to cover the filling, then fold it in half again to form a triangle or roll it into a cylinder.

Repeat the process with the remaining crepes and filling.

Serve the lemon blueberry mascarpone crepes warm, topped with fresh blueberries, a dusting of powdered sugar, and lemon zest for garnish.

Enjoy the delightful combination of tangy lemon, sweet blueberries, and creamy mascarpone wrapped in tender crepes—a perfect dessert for any occasion!

Apple Cinnamon Streusel Crepes

Ingredients:

For the crepes:

- 1 cup all-purpose flour
- 2 large eggs
- 1 1/4 cups whole milk
- 2 tablespoons unsalted butter, melted
- 2 tablespoons granulated sugar
- 1/2 teaspoon vanilla extract
- Pinch of salt
- Butter or oil, for cooking

For the apple filling:

- 2 large apples, peeled, cored, and thinly sliced
- 2 tablespoons unsalted butter
- 2 tablespoons brown sugar
- 1 teaspoon ground cinnamon
- 1/4 teaspoon ground nutmeg
- Pinch of salt

For the streusel topping:

- 1/4 cup all-purpose flour
- 1/4 cup rolled oats
- 2 tablespoons brown sugar
- 2 tablespoons unsalted butter, melted
- 1/2 teaspoon ground cinnamon

For serving:

- Powdered sugar for dusting
- Maple syrup or caramel sauce (optional)

Instructions:

In a large mixing bowl, whisk together the flour, eggs, milk, melted butter, sugar, vanilla extract, and salt until smooth. The batter should be thin and pourable. If it's too thick, you can add a bit more milk to reach the desired consistency.

Heat a non-stick skillet or crepe pan over medium heat. Add a small amount of butter or oil to the pan and swirl it around to coat the bottom evenly.

Once the pan is hot, pour about 1/4 cup of the crepe batter into the center of the pan. Quickly tilt and rotate the pan to spread the batter into a thin, even layer covering the bottom of the pan.

Cook the crepe for about 1-2 minutes, or until the edges start to lightly brown and lift away from the pan. Use a spatula to carefully flip the crepe over and cook for an additional 1-2 minutes on the other side, or until lightly golden.

Transfer the cooked crepe to a plate and set aside. Repeat with the remaining batter.

In a skillet, melt 2 tablespoons of unsalted butter over medium heat. Add the sliced apples, brown sugar, cinnamon, nutmeg, and a pinch of salt. Cook, stirring occasionally, until the apples are softened and caramelized, about 8-10 minutes. Remove from heat and set aside.

In a small bowl, mix together the streusel topping ingredients: flour, rolled oats, brown sugar, melted butter, and ground cinnamon until crumbly.

To assemble, spoon a portion of the apple filling onto one half of each crepe. Sprinkle a generous amount of streusel topping over the apple filling.

Fold the crepe in half to cover the filling, then fold it in half again to form a triangle or roll it into a cylinder.

Repeat the process with the remaining crepes and filling.

Serve the apple cinnamon streusel crepes warm, dusted with powdered sugar and drizzled with maple syrup or caramel sauce if desired.

Enjoy the comforting flavors of apple pie wrapped in tender crepes—a perfect breakfast or dessert treat!

Orange Creamsicle Crepes

Ingredients:

For the crepes:

- 1 cup all-purpose flour
- 2 large eggs
- 1 1/4 cups whole milk
- 2 tablespoons unsalted butter, melted
- 2 tablespoons granulated sugar
- Zest of 1 orange
- 1/2 teaspoon vanilla extract
- Pinch of salt
- Butter or oil, for cooking

For the orange cream filling:

- 1 cup heavy cream
- 2 tablespoons powdered sugar
- 1 teaspoon orange zest
- 1/2 teaspoon vanilla extract
- Orange food coloring (optional)

For serving:

- Fresh orange segments
- Powdered sugar for dusting
- Orange zest for garnish (optional)

Instructions:

In a large mixing bowl, whisk together the flour, eggs, milk, melted butter, sugar, orange zest, vanilla extract, and salt until smooth. The batter should be thin and pourable. If it's too thick, you can add a bit more milk to reach the desired consistency.

Heat a non-stick skillet or crepe pan over medium heat. Add a small amount of butter or oil to the pan and swirl it around to coat the bottom evenly.

Once the pan is hot, pour about 1/4 cup of the crepe batter into the center of the pan. Quickly tilt and rotate the pan to spread the batter into a thin, even layer covering the bottom of the pan.

Cook the crepe for about 1-2 minutes, or until the edges start to lightly brown and lift away from the pan. Use a spatula to carefully flip the crepe over and cook for an additional 1-2 minutes on the other side, or until lightly golden.

Transfer the cooked crepe to a plate and set aside. Repeat with the remaining batter.

In a mixing bowl, whip the heavy cream until it begins to thicken. Add the powdered sugar, orange zest, vanilla extract, and orange food coloring (if using). Continue to whip until soft peaks form.

To assemble, spread a generous portion of the orange cream filling onto one half of each crepe.

Fold the crepe in half to cover the filling, then fold it in half again to form a triangle or roll it into a cylinder.

Repeat the process with the remaining crepes and filling.

Serve the orange creamsicle crepes warm, topped with fresh orange segments, a dusting of powdered sugar, and orange zest for garnish if desired.

Enjoy the refreshing and creamy flavor of orange creamsicles wrapped in tender crepes—a delightful dessert reminiscent of childhood memories!

Hazelnut Espresso Crepes

Ingredients:

For the crepes:

- 1 cup all-purpose flour
- 2 large eggs
- 1 1/4 cups whole milk
- 2 tablespoons unsalted butter, melted
- 2 tablespoons granulated sugar
- 2 tablespoons hazelnut spread (such as Nutella)
- 1 tablespoon instant espresso powder
- Pinch of salt
- Butter or oil, for cooking

For the hazelnut espresso sauce:

- 1/2 cup heavy cream
- 2 tablespoons hazelnut spread (such as Nutella)
- 1 teaspoon instant espresso powder
- 1 tablespoon powdered sugar
- Chopped hazelnuts, for garnish (optional)

For serving:

- Whipped cream
- Chocolate shavings or cocoa powder (optional)

Instructions:

In a large mixing bowl, whisk together the flour, eggs, milk, melted butter, sugar, hazelnut spread, instant espresso powder, and salt until smooth. The batter should be thin and pourable. If it's too thick, you can add a bit more milk to reach the desired consistency.

Heat a non-stick skillet or crepe pan over medium heat. Add a small amount of butter or oil to the pan and swirl it around to coat the bottom evenly.

Once the pan is hot, pour about 1/4 cup of the crepe batter into the center of the pan. Quickly tilt and rotate the pan to spread the batter into a thin, even layer covering the bottom of the pan.

Cook the crepe for about 1-2 minutes, or until the edges start to lightly brown and lift away from the pan. Use a spatula to carefully flip the crepe over and cook for an additional 1-2 minutes on the other side, or until lightly golden.

Transfer the cooked crepe to a plate and set aside. Repeat with the remaining batter.

In a small saucepan, heat the heavy cream over medium-low heat until it just begins to simmer. Remove from heat and add the hazelnut spread, instant espresso powder, and powdered sugar. Stir until the hazelnut spread and espresso powder are completely dissolved and the mixture is smooth.

To assemble, fold each crepe into quarters and arrange them on serving plates. Drizzle the hazelnut espresso sauce over the folded crepes.

Top with a dollop of whipped cream and sprinkle with chopped hazelnuts and chocolate shavings or cocoa powder, if desired.

Serve the hazelnut espresso crepes warm, and enjoy the rich and indulgent flavor of hazelnut and espresso wrapped in tender crepes—a perfect dessert for coffee lovers!

Coconut Lime Crepes

Ingredients:

For the crepes:

- 1 cup all-purpose flour
- 2 large eggs
- 1 1/4 cups coconut milk
- 2 tablespoons unsalted butter, melted
- 2 tablespoons granulated sugar
- Zest of 1 lime
- 1 tablespoon lime juice
- Pinch of salt
- Butter or oil, for cooking

For the coconut lime filling:

- 1 cup shredded coconut
- 1/4 cup sweetened condensed milk
- Zest of 1 lime
- 1 tablespoon lime juice

For serving:

- Lime wedges
- Powdered sugar for dusting
- Toasted coconut flakes (optional)

Instructions:

In a large mixing bowl, whisk together the flour, eggs, coconut milk, melted butter, sugar, lime zest, lime juice, and salt until smooth. The batter should be thin and pourable. If it's too thick, you can add a bit more coconut milk to reach the desired consistency.

Heat a non-stick skillet or crepe pan over medium heat. Add a small amount of butter or oil to the pan and swirl it around to coat the bottom evenly.

Once the pan is hot, pour about 1/4 cup of the crepe batter into the center of the pan. Quickly tilt and rotate the pan to spread the batter into a thin, even layer covering the bottom of the pan.

Cook the crepe for about 1-2 minutes, or until the edges start to lightly brown and lift away from the pan. Use a spatula to carefully flip the crepe over and cook for an additional 1-2 minutes on the other side, or until lightly golden.

Transfer the cooked crepe to a plate and set aside. Repeat with the remaining batter.

In a mixing bowl, combine the shredded coconut, sweetened condensed milk, lime zest, and lime juice. Mix until well combined.

Spoon a portion of the coconut lime filling onto one half of each crepe.

Fold the crepe in half to cover the filling, then fold it in half again to form a triangle or roll it into a cylinder.

Repeat the process with the remaining crepes and filling.

Serve the coconut lime crepes warm, garnished with lime wedges, a dusting of powdered sugar, and toasted coconut flakes if desired.

Enjoy the tropical flavors of coconut and lime wrapped in tender crepes—a delightful dessert or breakfast option!

Pina Colada Crepes

Ingredients:

For the crepes:

- 1 cup all-purpose flour
- 2 large eggs
- 1 1/4 cups coconut milk
- 2 tablespoons unsalted butter, melted
- 2 tablespoons granulated sugar
- 1/2 teaspoon vanilla extract
- Pinch of salt
- Butter or oil, for cooking

For the pineapple-coconut filling:

- 1 cup diced pineapple
- 1/2 cup shredded coconut
- 2 tablespoons brown sugar
- 2 tablespoons rum (optional)
- 1 tablespoon unsalted butter

For the coconut whipped cream:

- 1 cup heavy cream
- 2 tablespoons powdered sugar
- 1/2 teaspoon coconut extract

For serving:

- Toasted coconut flakes
- Maraschino cherries

Instructions:

In a large mixing bowl, whisk together the flour, eggs, coconut milk, melted butter, sugar, vanilla extract, and salt until smooth. The batter should be thin and pourable. If it's too thick, you can add a bit more coconut milk to reach the desired consistency.

Heat a non-stick skillet or crepe pan over medium heat. Add a small amount of butter or oil to the pan and swirl it around to coat the bottom evenly.

Once the pan is hot, pour about 1/4 cup of the crepe batter into the center of the pan. Quickly tilt and rotate the pan to spread the batter into a thin, even layer covering the bottom of the pan.

Cook the crepe for about 1-2 minutes, or until the edges start to lightly brown and lift away from the pan. Use a spatula to carefully flip the crepe over and cook for an additional 1-2 minutes on the other side, or until lightly golden.

Transfer the cooked crepe to a plate and set aside. Repeat with the remaining batter.

In a skillet, melt the butter over medium heat. Add the diced pineapple and cook for 3-4 minutes, or until slightly caramelized. Add the shredded coconut, brown sugar, and rum (if using). Cook for an additional 2-3 minutes, stirring occasionally, until the mixture is heated through and the flavors are well combined. Remove from heat and set aside.

In a mixing bowl, whip the heavy cream until it begins to thicken. Add the powdered sugar and coconut extract, then continue to whip until soft peaks form.

To assemble, spoon a portion of the pineapple-coconut filling onto one half of each crepe.

Top with a dollop of coconut whipped cream.

Fold the crepe in half to cover the filling, then fold it in half again to form a triangle or roll it into a cylinder.

Repeat the process with the remaining crepes and filling.

Serve the Pina Colada crepes warm, garnished with toasted coconut flakes and a maraschino cherry on top.

Enjoy the tropical flavors of pineapple and coconut wrapped in tender crepes—a delightful dessert reminiscent of a classic Pina Colada cocktail!

Chocolate Cherry Cordial Crepes

Ingredients:

For the crepes:

- 1 cup all-purpose flour
- 2 large eggs
- 1 1/4 cups milk
- 2 tablespoons unsalted butter, melted
- 2 tablespoons granulated sugar
- 2 tablespoons cocoa powder
- 1/2 teaspoon vanilla extract
- Pinch of salt
- Butter or oil, for cooking

For the cherry filling:

- 1 cup pitted cherries, halved
- 2 tablespoons granulated sugar
- 1 tablespoon water
- 1 tablespoon cornstarch

For the chocolate sauce:

- 1/2 cup dark chocolate chips
- 1/4 cup heavy cream
- 1 tablespoon unsalted butter

For serving:

- Whipped cream
- Chocolate shavings or cocoa powder (optional)

Instructions:

In a large mixing bowl, whisk together the flour, eggs, milk, melted butter, sugar, cocoa powder, vanilla extract, and salt until smooth. The batter should be thin and pourable. If it's too thick, you can add a bit more milk to reach the desired consistency.

Heat a non-stick skillet or crepe pan over medium heat. Add a small amount of butter or oil to the pan and swirl it around to coat the bottom evenly.

Once the pan is hot, pour about 1/4 cup of the crepe batter into the center of the pan. Quickly tilt and rotate the pan to spread the batter into a thin, even layer covering the bottom of the pan.

Cook the crepe for about 1-2 minutes, or until the edges start to lightly brown and lift away from the pan. Use a spatula to carefully flip the crepe over and cook for an additional 1-2 minutes on the other side, or until lightly golden.

Transfer the cooked crepe to a plate and set aside. Repeat with the remaining batter.

In a saucepan, combine the pitted cherries, granulated sugar, water, and cornstarch. Cook over medium heat, stirring occasionally, until the cherries soften and release their juices, and the mixture thickens slightly, about 5-7 minutes. Remove from heat and set aside.

In another saucepan, heat the heavy cream until it just begins to simmer. Remove from heat and add the dark chocolate chips and unsalted butter. Let it sit for a minute, then stir until the chocolate is completely melted and the mixture is smooth.

To assemble, spoon a portion of the cherry filling onto one half of each crepe. Drizzle some of the chocolate sauce over the cherry filling.

Fold the crepe in half to cover the filling, then fold it in half again to form a triangle or roll it into a cylinder.

Repeat the process with the remaining crepes and filling.

Serve the chocolate cherry cordial crepes warm, topped with whipped cream and chocolate shavings or cocoa powder if desired.

Enjoy the indulgent flavors of chocolate and cherries wrapped in tender crepes—a perfect dessert for any chocolate lover!

Cranberry Orange Crepes

Ingredients:

For the crepes:

- 1 cup all-purpose flour
- 2 large eggs
- 1 1/4 cups milk
- 2 tablespoons unsalted butter, melted
- 2 tablespoons granulated sugar
- Zest of 1 orange
- 1 tablespoon orange juice
- 1/2 teaspoon vanilla extract
- Pinch of salt
- Butter or oil, for cooking

For the cranberry-orange compote:

- 1 cup fresh cranberries
- 1/4 cup orange juice
- 1/4 cup granulated sugar
- Zest of 1 orange

For serving:

- Powdered sugar
- Orange zest for garnish
- Whipped cream or vanilla ice cream (optional)

Instructions:

In a large mixing bowl, whisk together the flour, eggs, milk, melted butter, sugar, orange zest, orange juice, vanilla extract, and salt until smooth. The batter should be thin and pourable. If it's too thick, you can add a bit more milk to reach the desired consistency.

Heat a non-stick skillet or crepe pan over medium heat. Add a small amount of butter or oil to the pan and swirl it around to coat the bottom evenly.

Once the pan is hot, pour about 1/4 cup of the crepe batter into the center of the pan. Quickly tilt and rotate the pan to spread the batter into a thin, even layer covering the bottom of the pan.

Cook the crepe for about 1-2 minutes, or until the edges start to lightly brown and lift away from the pan. Use a spatula to carefully flip the crepe over and cook for an additional 1-2 minutes on the other side, or until lightly golden.

Transfer the cooked crepe to a plate and set aside. Repeat with the remaining batter.

In a saucepan, combine the fresh cranberries, orange juice, granulated sugar, and orange zest. Cook over medium heat, stirring occasionally, until the cranberries burst and release their juices, and the mixture thickens slightly, about 5-7 minutes. Remove from heat and set aside.

To assemble, spoon a portion of the cranberry-orange compote onto one half of each crepe.

Fold the crepe in half to cover the filling, then fold it in half again to form a triangle or roll it into a cylinder.

Repeat the process with the remaining crepes and filling.

Serve the cranberry orange crepes warm, dusted with powdered sugar and garnished with orange zest.

Optionally, serve with whipped cream or vanilla ice cream on the side.

Enjoy the delightful combination of tangy cranberries and zesty orange wrapped in tender crepes—a perfect treat for breakfast or dessert!

Almond Joy Crepes

Ingredients:

For the crepes:

- 1 cup all-purpose flour
- 2 large eggs
- 1 1/4 cups milk
- 2 tablespoons unsalted butter, melted
- 2 tablespoons granulated sugar
- 1/2 teaspoon vanilla extract
- Pinch of salt
- Butter or oil, for cooking

For the coconut filling:

- 1 cup shredded coconut
- 1/4 cup sweetened condensed milk
- 1/4 cup chopped almonds
- 1/4 cup mini chocolate chips

For serving:

- Chocolate syrup
- Toasted almonds
- Shredded coconut

Instructions:

In a large mixing bowl, whisk together the flour, eggs, milk, melted butter, sugar, vanilla extract, and salt until smooth. The batter should be thin and pourable. If it's too thick, you can add a bit more milk to reach the desired consistency.
Heat a non-stick skillet or crepe pan over medium heat. Add a small amount of butter or oil to the pan and swirl it around to coat the bottom evenly.
Once the pan is hot, pour about 1/4 cup of the crepe batter into the center of the pan. Quickly tilt and rotate the pan to spread the batter into a thin, even layer covering the bottom of the pan.

Cook the crepe for about 1-2 minutes, or until the edges start to lightly brown and lift away from the pan. Use a spatula to carefully flip the crepe over and cook for an additional 1-2 minutes on the other side, or until lightly golden.

Transfer the cooked crepe to a plate and set aside. Repeat with the remaining batter.

In a mixing bowl, combine the shredded coconut, sweetened condensed milk, chopped almonds, and mini chocolate chips. Mix until well combined.

To assemble, spoon a portion of the coconut filling onto one half of each crepe. Fold the crepe in half to cover the filling, then fold it in half again to form a triangle or roll it into a cylinder.

Repeat the process with the remaining crepes and filling.

Serve the Almond Joy crepes warm, drizzled with chocolate syrup and topped with toasted almonds and shredded coconut.

Enjoy the delicious flavors of coconut, almonds, and chocolate wrapped in tender crepes—a perfect dessert reminiscent of the classic candy bar!

Raspberry Lemon Cheesecake Crepes

Ingredients:

For the crepes:

- 1 cup all-purpose flour
- 2 large eggs
- 1 1/4 cups milk
- 2 tablespoons unsalted butter, melted
- 2 tablespoons granulated sugar
- Zest of 1 lemon
- 1/2 teaspoon vanilla extract
- Pinch of salt
- Butter or oil, for cooking

For the raspberry filling:

- 1 cup fresh raspberries
- 2 tablespoons granulated sugar
- 1 tablespoon lemon juice

For the lemon cheesecake filling:

- 8 oz (225g) cream cheese, softened
- 1/4 cup powdered sugar
- Zest of 1 lemon
- 1 tablespoon lemon juice
- 1/2 teaspoon vanilla extract

For serving:

- Fresh raspberries
- Powdered sugar for dusting
- Lemon zest for garnish

Instructions:

In a large mixing bowl, whisk together the flour, eggs, milk, melted butter, sugar, lemon zest, vanilla extract, and salt until smooth. The batter should be thin and pourable. If it's too thick, you can add a bit more milk to reach the desired consistency.

Heat a non-stick skillet or crepe pan over medium heat. Add a small amount of butter or oil to the pan and swirl it around to coat the bottom evenly.

Once the pan is hot, pour about 1/4 cup of the crepe batter into the center of the pan. Quickly tilt and rotate the pan to spread the batter into a thin, even layer covering the bottom of the pan.

Cook the crepe for about 1-2 minutes, or until the edges start to lightly brown and lift away from the pan. Use a spatula to carefully flip the crepe over and cook for an additional 1-2 minutes on the other side, or until lightly golden.

Transfer the cooked crepe to a plate and set aside. Repeat with the remaining batter.

In a saucepan, combine the fresh raspberries, granulated sugar, and lemon juice. Cook over medium heat, stirring occasionally, until the raspberries break down and the mixture thickens slightly, about 5-7 minutes. Remove from heat and set aside.

In a mixing bowl, beat the softened cream cheese, powdered sugar, lemon zest, lemon juice, and vanilla extract until smooth and creamy.

To assemble, spread a generous portion of the lemon cheesecake filling onto one half of each crepe.

Spoon some of the raspberry filling over the lemon cheesecake filling.

Fold the crepe in half to cover the filling, then fold it in half again to form a triangle or roll it into a cylinder.

Repeat the process with the remaining crepes and filling.

Serve the raspberry lemon cheesecake crepes warm, topped with fresh raspberries, a dusting of powdered sugar, and lemon zest for garnish.

Enjoy the delightful combination of tangy lemon cheesecake and sweet raspberry wrapped in tender crepes—a perfect dessert for any occasion!

Chocolate Mint Crepes

Ingredients:

For the crepes:

- 1 cup all-purpose flour
- 2 large eggs
- 1 1/4 cups milk
- 2 tablespoons unsalted butter, melted
- 2 tablespoons granulated sugar
- 2 tablespoons cocoa powder
- 1/2 teaspoon vanilla extract
- Pinch of salt
- Butter or oil, for cooking

For the mint chocolate filling:

- 1 cup heavy cream
- 1/4 cup powdered sugar
- 1/2 teaspoon peppermint extract
- Green food coloring (optional)
- 1/2 cup chocolate chips, melted

For serving:

- Chocolate syrup
- Fresh mint leaves (optional)

Instructions:

In a large mixing bowl, whisk together the flour, eggs, milk, melted butter, sugar, cocoa powder, vanilla extract, and salt until smooth. The batter should be thin and pourable. If it's too thick, you can add a bit more milk to reach the desired consistency.

Heat a non-stick skillet or crepe pan over medium heat. Add a small amount of butter or oil to the pan and swirl it around to coat the bottom evenly.

Once the pan is hot, pour about 1/4 cup of the crepe batter into the center of the pan. Quickly tilt and rotate the pan to spread the batter into a thin, even layer covering the bottom of the pan.

Cook the crepe for about 1-2 minutes, or until the edges start to lightly brown and lift away from the pan. Use a spatula to carefully flip the crepe over and cook for an additional 1-2 minutes on the other side, or until lightly golden.

Transfer the cooked crepe to a plate and set aside. Repeat with the remaining batter.

In a mixing bowl, whip the heavy cream until it begins to thicken. Add the powdered sugar, peppermint extract, and green food coloring (if using). Continue to whip until soft peaks form.

Gently fold in the melted chocolate chips until well combined.

To assemble, spoon a portion of the mint chocolate filling onto one half of each crepe.

Fold the crepe in half to cover the filling, then fold it in half again to form a triangle or roll it into a cylinder.

Repeat the process with the remaining crepes and filling.

Serve the chocolate mint crepes warm, drizzled with chocolate syrup and garnished with fresh mint leaves if desired.

Enjoy the irresistible combination of rich chocolate and refreshing mint wrapped in tender crepes—a perfect dessert for chocolate lovers!

White Chocolate Raspberry Crepes

Ingredients:

For the crepes:

- 1 cup all-purpose flour
- 2 large eggs
- 1 1/4 cups milk
- 2 tablespoons unsalted butter, melted
- 2 tablespoons granulated sugar
- 1/2 teaspoon vanilla extract
- Pinch of salt
- Butter or oil, for cooking

For the white chocolate filling:

- 4 oz (115g) white chocolate, chopped
- 1/2 cup heavy cream
- 1/2 teaspoon vanilla extract

For the raspberry sauce:

- 1 cup fresh raspberries
- 2 tablespoons granulated sugar
- 1 tablespoon lemon juice

For serving:

- Fresh raspberries
- Powdered sugar for dusting

Instructions:

In a large mixing bowl, whisk together the flour, eggs, milk, melted butter, sugar, vanilla extract, and salt until smooth. The batter should be thin and pourable. If it's too thick, you can add a bit more milk to reach the desired consistency.

Heat a non-stick skillet or crepe pan over medium heat. Add a small amount of butter or oil to the pan and swirl it around to coat the bottom evenly.

Once the pan is hot, pour about 1/4 cup of the crepe batter into the center of the pan. Quickly tilt and rotate the pan to spread the batter into a thin, even layer covering the bottom of the pan.

Cook the crepe for about 1-2 minutes, or until the edges start to lightly brown and lift away from the pan. Use a spatula to carefully flip the crepe over and cook for an additional 1-2 minutes on the other side, or until lightly golden.

Transfer the cooked crepe to a plate and set aside. Repeat with the remaining batter.

In a small saucepan, heat the heavy cream over medium heat until it just begins to simmer. Remove from heat and add the chopped white chocolate and vanilla extract. Let it sit for a minute, then stir until the white chocolate is completely melted and the mixture is smooth.

In another saucepan, combine the fresh raspberries, granulated sugar, and lemon juice. Cook over medium heat, stirring occasionally, until the raspberries break down and the mixture thickens slightly, about 5-7 minutes. Remove from heat and set aside.

To assemble, spoon a portion of the white chocolate filling onto one half of each crepe.

Spoon some of the raspberry sauce over the white chocolate filling.

Fold the crepe in half to cover the filling, then fold it in half again to form a triangle or roll it into a cylinder.

Repeat the process with the remaining crepes and filling.

Serve the white chocolate raspberry crepes warm, topped with fresh raspberries and a dusting of powdered sugar.

Enjoy the decadent combination of creamy white chocolate and tart raspberries wrapped in tender crepes—a perfect dessert for any occasion!

www.ingramcontent.com/pod-product-compliance
Lightning Source LLC
LaVergne TN
LVHW081559060526
838201LV00054B/1980